LABOR TRAINING IN DEVELOPING COUNTRIES

LABOR TRAINING IN DEVELOPING COUNTRIES

A Challenge in Responsible Democracy

ARNOLD ZACK

With a Foreword by William Y. Elliott

FREDERICK A. PRAEGER, *Publisher*
New York · London

FREDERICK A. PRAEGER, PUBLISHER
64 UNIVERSITY PLACE, NEW YORK 3, N.Y., U.S.A.
77–79 CHARLOTTE STREET, LONDON W. 1, ENGLAND

Published in the United States of America in 1964
by Frederick A. Praeger, Inc., Publisher

Library of Congress Catalog Card Number: 64-13493

Printed in the United States of America

FOREWORD

Arnold Zack, a successful lawyer and labor arbitrator who is now a Fulbright Professor in labor relations at Haile Selassie I University in Addis Ababa, worked with me for two years in a seminar on Educational Training for the Developing Countries at Harvard University's Littauer School for Public Administration. Partly as a result of the work he did in that seminar, and with the additional advantage of several field trips—to Africa, and to parts of Asia, the Middle East, Europe, and the Caribbean—he has written this study on labor training in developing countries. There are a number of more specialized studies, but none, I think, that focuses so directly on the connection of labor training with responsible democracy.

Mr. Zack's book shows that the world labor movement—in particular, the American labor movement—has had to learn some new lessons on the role of organized labor in the world that is emerging with the disappearance of colonial control. In many of the new countries, the primary problem today is not simply one of forcing up wages while trying to secure the most advantageous treatment for the unions. While the systems of government in emerging and developing countries vary tremendously, the government is, directly or indirectly, the principal employer of labor in most cases, and the first problem is that of achieving a political organization and economic balance that will permit the nation to be self-sustaining: Education in responsibility and in a feeling of partnership for the fate of the country is the first requirement.

In advanced countries, there are many critics of trade unionism who feel that union policies are often, like those

v

of the medieval guilds, too restrictive; or, unlike the guilds, not as concerned with the quality and growth of output or the adequacy of technical training as they should be. This is too sweeping a judgment of the union movement, and in many parts of the world there are honorable exceptions to this rule. It is nevertheless true that when trade unions began to look at what the role of labor in the new countries would be, they found an opportunity for labor education along different lines which the American unions were, in many cases, ill prepared to fill, and for which the European unions, especially in countries like France, were even less well suited. The backgrounds of some unions, like those of the nonfederal government employees in the United States, were more suitable for the tremendous assistance the union movement was uniquely qualified to offer—both because of their sympathy for the unions they fostered and because of the acceptance accorded them by the recipients.

This study, as Mr. Zack honestly admits, only opens the door to the major problems, by showing how some typical efforts at assistance in labor training have worked—the setting up of a labor college at Kampala, and efforts made at centers in Puerto Rico, Tel Aviv, Geneva, Mexico City, Washington, Calcutta, and the Philippines. Surely, there is much relevant and useful material in the accounts of these experiences that Mr. Zack's book contains. The book's most valuable feature, however, is that Mr. Zack raises the question of the unions' responsibility for encouraging another and different kind of participation by labor in national life—the support of constitutional governments (even those whose life hangs daily in the balance, as in Venezuela)—a support that must be developed in trade-union indoctrination. Combining the forces of business, governmental, and other employees in the needed task of maintaining and supporting regimes that are aimed at responsible constitutional development may make possible the conditions under which constructive and free trade unions can exist and develop.

This kind of tripartite approach (labor, management, and

government) indicates a new attitude on the part of organized labor which augurs well for a type of statesmanship compatible with the great opportunities for creative and constructive leadership in the new countries.

Mr. Zack's appendixes are particularly useful, for they provide a background against which to judge the magnitude of the problems and the prospects for their solution.

Unfortunately, none of the international meetings devoted to these problems, including that sponsored by the Peace Corps in Puerto Rico in October of 1963, has yet produced the kind of support necessary to consolidate or even coordinate programs of training assistance in the various nations or labor movements. In the United States, the Agency for International Development and the Peace Corps have made valuable contributions, but in community development and the enlistment of voluntary services of world-wide free trade-union movements, there is much left to be done, and even more to be hoped and worked for. The virtue of Mr. Zack's book is that it is written by a man who has well-balanced sympathy for the free labor movement and is uniquely well versed in the problems and the opportunities for tackling this high-priority job in the education of the new nations—namely, training for responsible development, in politics as well as in economics.

—William Y. Elliott
Williams Professor of History and Politics, Emeritus,
Harvard University
University Professor, The American University,
Washington, D.C.

AUTHOR'S PREFACE

This volume has been written as a result of several trips abroad to study labor relations in general, and systems of voluntary dispute settlement in particular. I came to realize that rational systems of resolving industrial conflict would be unattainable until the trade unions developed responsible leaders who were stable enough effectively to negotiate such procedures on a par with their counterparts in management. Subsequent research into the efforts being made to develop trade-union leadership in the United States and in other countries revealed a lack of literature in this all-important field and the great need for detailed study of existing programs, if the various efforts to stimulate union leadership were to profit from the experience of others elsewhere in the world. Above all, the research brought home to me the need to inform trade unionists, management, and the public in industrialized nations of the efforts made in this field. This is particularly important not only in achieving wide-spread acceptance of the trade unions in new nations, but also for encouraging their activities as autonomous democratic institutions partaking in national development. The tendency for newly established governments to absorb trade-union leaders, and to manipulate the unions for the nation's political and economic purposes rather than to encourage them for the benefit of the rank-and-file citizenry, makes it all the more important to explain the nature of labor training.

This study is an attempt to shed some light on various international efforts in trade-union development. The benefits that may be gained from it are largely due to the cooperation extended to me by the administrators and staffs of the various centers I studied; my efforts were limited to reporting on and evaluating their experiences. I am particularly grateful for their kindness and interest, their patient tolerance of my ignorance, and the help they gave me in conversation and subsequent correspondence. Dr. Cicero Calderon of the Asian Labor Education Center; V. S. Mathur of the Asian Trade Union College; R. S. Mehta, Joint Secretary of the Indian Department of Labor and Employment; Joseph Odero-Jowi of the Kampala Labor College; Judith Simhoni of Israel's Histadrut; Thomas Miller of the American Institute of Free Labor Development; Amir Ali of the ILO Institute; and Miles Galvin of the University of Puerto Rico were all most gracious hosts, and, together with Morris Paladino of ORIT, were kind enough to read and criticize the manuscript. I am also grateful to David Morse, Albert Guigui, and Paul Chu of the International Labor Office for their continued encouragement and assistance; to Arnold Steinbach and Daniel Lazorchick of the Department of Labor, and George P. Delaney of the Department of State, for their help in establishing many of my initial contacts and for their continued cooperation; and especially to Herbert Tulatz of the ICFTU, who made many valuable personal and professional suggestions in the course of my study.

I am grateful to Mrs. Hilda O'Farrell and Miss Margaret Connell for their secretarial assistance; to Arnold Dolin for his editorial advice; and to Isaac Patch for the hospitality he extended me during much of the writing.

Thanks are due also to my arbitration colleague, Saul Wallen, who offered unfailing encouragement, and without whose tolerance none of my efforts in this or other fields would have succeeded.

Finally, I wish to offer my deepest thanks to Dr. William Y. Elliott, of Harvard University, who not only stimulated the idea of this study, but—with the cooperation of Don Price, Dean of the Graduate School of Public Administration of Harvard University—made possible its completion and publication through a grant from the resources of the research seminar on University–Governmental Relations in Educational Training for Underdeveloped Areas. It is he who is primarily responsible for any contribution this book may make to the field of labor leadership training.

—A. Z.

Addis Ababa, Ethiopia
November, 1963

CONTENTS

Contents

LABOR TRAINING
IN DEVELOPING
COUNTRIES

Achieving the objectives of Latin America and the rest of the Free World requires the support of the workers and their trade unions in these countries. Support will be forthcoming only when workers have opportunity for full participation in the affairs of the nation. Effective and responsible leaders are essential in gaining the participation of the unions in the social and economic life of these nations and in making such participation meaningful to workers.

—President JOHN F. KENNEDY, *in a letter to J. Peter Grace, Jr., Chairman of the Board of the American Institute for Free Labor Development, January 18, 1962*

1. WHY TRADE-UNION DEVELOPMENT?

Economic development has become a byword of the mid-twentieth century. Virtually everyone is concerned with some facet of the world-wide effort to raise the living standards of the developing nations of Africa, Asia, and Latin America. A most important component of the expanding economies of these nations is the increase in trade-union activity. Prior to World War II, trade unions in these countries were generally either nonexistent or virtually powerless. But now they are attaining much greater stature and significance, and their development has become the object of widespread international interest and concern.

What accounts for this recent upsurge in the awareness of and growth in trade unions of developing nations? The answer can be found in economic, social, and political factors.

Considered from an economic viewpoint, trade-union development may be traced to a rapidly growing world trade, in which ever-increasing industrialization creates a demand for more and more materials and inputs, thus stimulating an ever-widening market for its products and output. This necessitates the expansion of commercial and governmental activity in areas of the world that were previously in a subsistence category, far removed from the economic or trade sphere. This change brings growth to the local economy, creating new jobs and attracting new laborers into the workforce. Because of its subsistence background, this new workforce is often unaware of how to attain a just share of the wealth it produces and logically turns to trade unions for protection and representation in its efforts to attain more advantageous wages, hours, and working conditions. The growth of trade unions may, in turn, contribute to economic development by stabilizing the workforce, providing training for the workers, and as a source to instill in them a sense of their responsibilities in the development of their nation.

From a social viewpoint, enlargement of the economies and expansion of the workforces have attracted untrained and uneducated laborers from the agricultural and rural sectors of the economy. Realizing the disadvantages of illiteracy and intellectual backwardness, they turn quickly to whatever structures are available for education and training to improve their standing as citizens of the community. Few governments provide such educational opportunities for their urbanizing citizens. Some training in skills is usually offered by employers. However, the absence of preconditioning for skill training—simple literacy skills and basic academic education—accentuates the difficulties of such workers in adapting to their new surroundings. If trade unions offer them a hope of overcoming these personal deficiencies, they are deluged with new members.

As for the political causes, it should be remembered that the Charter of the United Nations committed its members to the achievement of self-determination and self-government for all peoples in the former colonial areas. While this was important in Africa and Asia, the goal of self-government was less meaningful for Latin America, where colonial rule had, by and large, ended in the nineteenth century. Yet there are great similarities in the situation of the trade unionists in all three continents. They constitute a new urbanizing or modernizing segment of society, made up of those who were hitherto deprived of any opportunity for advancement and of any right to determine their own futures in the political arena. Now they have begun to sense their new power and a world-wide audience that is increasingly sympathetic to their efforts. This is true for Latin Americans as well as Africans and Asians. The colonial governments neglected to provide educational opportunities by which the workers could advance into new positions or raise voices that could be heard. For the worker interested in expressing himself, it was only logical that he turn to the one organization interested in "taking his side." Clearly, the trade union was the only institution readily available to him. Although trade unions function primarily as an economic force, it cannot be denied that in developing areas they also constitute an important source of political strength.

In the period of colonialism, trade unions frequently provided the needed base for national independence movements. Because of their financial independence, large membership, and ready-made, nation-wide structure for rallying political support in both urban and rural areas, they became natural allies to nationalist movements, which were frequently prohibited by colonial governments. Their political importance is even greater in the post-independence period, because they constitute the most important institution in the new nations with influence and support among that segment of the population most interested in political life. Their members come from a social group that has made the commitment to self-advancement and participation in economic development by turning to wage employment; they are also the voters who may shape the political futures of these countries.

As institutions, the trade unions have an economic influence that can be used to interfere with, or support, the government programs for rapid national development. The extent to which they participate affirmatively in economic development depends on the respect they are accorded by the national governments, which may find it convenient in the short run to discourage trade-union autonomy, and on their ability to demonstrate that they are in unity with the government in seeking a better way of life for all citizens. The effectiveness of their efforts will depend on whether they can stimulate a sense of national pride and trade-union loyalty among their members. Without doubt, trade unions can make an enormous contribution to national development and responsible national leadership. They are the only institutions that have the means to teach practical and functional democracy to a great segment of the population. They can do this by involving the members in the union activities, through programs of education of the rank and file, and—in their daily operations—through demonstrations of loyalty to democratic principles and to autonomous trade unionism. In short, trade unions are important politically because of their potential for teaching responsible democracy to the most influential segments of the new nations.

For these reasons, the growth of trade unions in Asia, Africa, and Latin America poses a challenge to labor organizations and governments alike in the more advanced industrial countries of the world. The question has become: What, if any, part should we in the advanced countries, particularly the United States, play in the development of trade unionism in the new nations? The answer varies, of course, with the background and orientation of the party that responds.

The response of the trade unionist would vary with the intensity of his devotion to the movement. The apathetic trade unionist neither knows nor cares about the problems of trade unions in other countries. There is a more active but nationalist type of trade unionist, who takes a protectionist or even isolationist attitude when approached on the subject of foreign economic relations. On the whole, however, it is fair to say that the active trade unionist, particularly when informed of the role of trade unions abroad, views their strengthening and development as indispensable to the attainment of a higher standard of living. He would seek to provide whatever technical assistance could be made available to make them stronger, economically more effective, able to challenge the unilateral power of employers (public or private) and exert pressure on them sufficient to raise wages, reduce work hours, and improve working conditions.

The response of the employer might be more negative. Although there are still many employers in the United States who feel that their situation would be better if there were no trade unions at all, most employers accept the existence of responsible unions, although they may challenge their actions in specific instances. They have accepted the moral justification of group protection of the rights of the individual worker, and seek to develop relations with the union that will constitute an effective channel of communication to the worker and a means of ascertaining and solving problems in business operations. Both groups of employers would probably transfer their domestic attitudes to the foreign context when answering the question of the community's proper role in trade-union activities abroad. Some might view intensified trade-union activity abroad as a means of raising wages in foreign countries, thus decreasing the disparity in labor costs between American and overseas industry. Some might argue that trade unions are necessary to protect the individual worker against neocolonial exploitation, particularly after generations of subservience to the unilateral power of the employer.

In this connection, I was interested to note the attitude toward trade unions of employers in Africa. In one instance, I had given a speech before a group of white employers in the Copper Belt of Northern Rhodesia on the subject of voluntary arbitration in the United States. An owner of a large laundry concern asked if I knew the proper African trade-union official to approach about organizing his employees. After I had indicated my surprise at this request, the owner pointed out that his managerial staff were all white, and his laborers all black. Because of this, any reprimand of the employees, however just, was labeled as racial bigotry. The employer wanted a responsible union representing the employees to assist in maintaining reasonable discipline, provide him with a means of overcoming the race barrier, and give him a centralized body of labor opinion with which to negotiate.

A second incident occurred in the Western Region of the Cameroons a few days before its merger with its French-speaking neighbor. The writer was attending a meeting of local plantation workers, who were discussing a series of recommendations for an initial collective-bargaining agreement offered by their employer. The benefits were liberal and the protections offered to the employees and the union quite significant. A visit to the personnel director for the employer proved that no strings were attached. They were trying to build a strong union. Why? The management official reasoned as follows: "Our employees are good workers, sincere and loyal. They have asked for recognition of their union, and it should prove to be a responsible one. Next week, this territory will become part of the Republic of Cameroon, where the unions are run politically, and filled with radicals. Those radicals have turned legitimate organizations into political units whose main objective is to cause trouble. If we can develop a strong, independent, and democratic union here before the Communists start to operate, then we shall be protected from disruption and perhaps takeover by them. In addition, our employees will be sure that their union will not be subverted and destroyed."

These two incidents do not necessarily represent universal management reaction to trade unions in Africa or anywhere else. But they indicate certain virtues of trade unions that are often taken for granted in more industrialized nations, where they have functioned for more than two centuries. Quite a different response is likely to come from the public at large. In many cases, of course, the public view would reflect the labor or management attitudes indicated above. But it is more likely to indicate the increasing realization of the alert citizenry in the West that the long-suffering "underdog" in less developed areas has a legitimate claim to a higher standard of living and to protection against continued suppression by his employer. This rather theoretical attitude would support trade-union development not only on economic grounds but on political and perhaps social and educational grounds as well. In other words, the trade unions are coming to be known as dynamic forces in the movement toward independence, as spawning grounds for political leaders, and as a means to provide education and training for the rank and file in their responsibilities in the new societies. According to this reasoning, trade unions per se deserve support and sustenance from the more developed countries.

Finally, we should consider the attitudes of the governments of industrialized countries toward trade unions in the new nations. Those attitudes are of utmost importance both philosophically, in terms of the roles of government and private institutions, and practically, in view of the power position of unions vis-à-vis the governments of the new countries, and the wealth of resources at their command.

Obviously, a government should represent the views of all three groups: labor, management, and the public. In addition, it must weigh other considerations on a more practical, or pragmatic, basis than the private sector. Let us confine ourselves to several problems facing the United States Government, in considering its proper role in international labor.

The first problem is one of reconciling the government's stimulation of foreign trade unions with its hands-off policy toward trade unions in this country. It can be argued that the Federal Government has generally remained aloof from labor relations in the United States, offering its services as a regulatory device rather than as a stimulant or depressant to trade-union growth. Nonetheless, it would be difficult to prove that the Federal Government did not stimulate trade-union growth outright with the passage and enforcement of the original National Labor Relations Act (the Wagner-Connery Act), or that any government regulatory action at the present time, with our precarious balance in labor-management relations, would neither help nor harm the union. Can the U.S. Government, entrusted with maintaining a balance between labor and management in this country, plunge into the fray on the labor side overseas? If it does, can it make use of U.S. trade-union personnel or facilities without becoming indebted to them at home for their support and assistance abroad?

This leads to the second problem, that of relations between the American Government and American business concerns abroad. With our expanding business activities abroad, can the U.S. Government undertake a program of trade-union stimulation that will inevitably result in its supporting, at least by implication, the union side in the labor-management balance? Could this not result in support of a foreign trade union in its organizational drive against an American corporation abroad?

The third concern is that of the proper role of the U.S. Government in relation to the governments of developing countries and their former colonial rulers. We have frequently extolled our support of movements of independence in Asia and Africa, and given significant moral and material support to back up our statements. But we have perhaps even more frequently refrained from providing much more than lip service if it was felt that our actions would involve us in difficulties with the area's former ruling powers, who frequently are our allies in other areas. This problem is particularly troublesome if the government of the developing nation is seeking to destroy the autonomy and independence of the local trade-union movement.

The fourth problem is probably the most difficult. It concerns the often conflicting goals of economic development and trade-union development. Those in favor of the most rapid achievement of economic development claim that total support of the objective is required. They stress the importance of unified action to fulfill government plans, the ease with which total community participation in the development programs can be attained, and the need for the full cooperation of the trade-union movement. Too often, they minimize the likely threats to individual freedom and to the right to protest against unjustified government actions. Indeed, there is also a school of thought that fears that a total commitment to development may result in extreme government control and elimination of institutions founded on free expression and self-government. This school is concerned with the development of democratic institutions pledged to protect individual rights and seeks to assure their place and right to action as fundamental to the economy and polity they are building. These two theories need not be contradictory. But there is a strong likelihood that the entrepreneurial role of the government of a developing country will conflict with those groups demanding a higher return for their labor (and a reduced profit available for reinvestment).

Where do the U.S. Government's interests properly belong in this dilemma? Should we place assistance in economic development so high on our list of priorities that we perforce encourage the introduction of controls over those institutions committed to practical democracy and freedom of expression? Or should we actively support those forces that seek to strengthen the ideals in which we believe, while at the same time they seek to secure a larger share of the available pie —higher per capita income and better working conditions— thus limiting the prospects of most rapid economic growth because of reduced profits? The problem is heightened in those nations where the government acts directly as employer and encourages support for its program on political as well as economic grounds.

There are many arguments advanced on the virtue of securing a wide voluntary institutional base, such as that provided by trade-unions and cooperatives, in these countries. Certainly, there is merit in the view that democracy, once suppressed by strict governmental control, has little likelihood of rapid or effective re-establishment. Similarly, there is much sense in the argument that the pace of economic development might be stimulated more by heavy excise or personal income taxes and a larger per capita income than by the present reliance on management's return from investment—particularly in nations with an inefficient tax or financial structure that permits a heavy outflow of profit by a small expatriate business-owning clique, who more often than not refuse to reinvest their profits where earned. An effective trade union, then, might do much to stimulate economic development rather than retard it.

A fifth concern is the importance of trade unions in many developing areas as a spawning ground for political leaders.

There is no doubt of the need for trained leadership in many parts of Africa, and elsewhere. And trade unions in the developing nations are much more than merely economic organs. Whether their leaders have joined the trade-union movement out of idealism or self-interest, the fact remains that trade-union leaders do go into politics, or at least constitute an important force in political as well as economic affairs, in their own countries and internationally. There are a large number of political leaders, particularly in Africa, who moved to high government authority from the trade-union movement. Trade unions are often the only available institution in which a natural leader may rise to political prominence while keeping his necessary "grass-roots" contacts. We are all aware, for instance, of the paucity of educational facilities available in Africa to those lacking personal wealth or family prestige. A few individuals are able to secure an advanced academic education, and they are frequently attracted to the prestige clerical and administrative jobs formerly reserved to colonialists, thus becoming part of the "elite" in the civil service or commercial administration. A few others succeed, by virtue of practical business sense and hard work, in breaking the European monopoly of business enterprises, and achieve leading positions in the economic community. Both types of successful Africans have achieved personal success at the expense of losing their contact with their own society and, indeed, may outdo the colonialists in antagonism toward the masses. But the African aspiring to politics, lacking formal education but still seeking advancement, cannot tread this road. His need is for a formal structure to assist his rise to leadership, status, and prestige that still permits him to maintain his roots among the people, a necessity for political success. The structure that best suits him is the trade union. There is scarcely a country in Africa today that does not boast of political leaders with a trade-union background. Tom Mboya of Kenya, Rachidi Kawawa of Tanganyika, Cyrille Adoula of the Congo, Joshua Nkomo of Southern Rhodesia, and Sékou Touré of Guinea are but a few.

The need for leadership and administrative skills in the

newly emerging countries is clear. The vacuum created by the departure of colonial governments and the failure to train their successors in administration and government operation make even greater the responsibilities placed on those few organizations that do train leaders, such as cooperatives and trade unions. The United States must consider the extent to which it may wish to support trade-union programs that stimulate the development of further leadership. For, in addition to the technical and administrative experience acquired in the trade unions, there is great political value in the exposure to its functioning democracy, responsive to the will of the majority.

Until we have faith in the ability of indigenous democratic organizations to develop responsive and responsible political leaders, we shall have to continue to work with leaders that may violate our standards of democracy, solely because they are readily available, even though they may not truly represent the will of their constituents. The development of grass-roots democracy through stimulation of independent trade unions might protect us and the citizens of these countries against the rise of totalitarian leadership in future years.

Underlying these five problems is a single need: Something must be done to stimulate in the rank and file an awareness of responsibilities and potentials as actively participating citizens in the emerging nations. The role of any government in this field is a difficult one, and the evidence certainly does not point to any clear-cut path to the desired goal. Regardless of the labor, management, public, or government viewpoint, the fact remains that trade unions are an instrumental force in the new nations, and if any basic tenet is the key one, it is that education and training are essential. It is the purpose of this volume to examine several international programs of education and training in the trade-union context, in order to learn what is being done, what motivates the sponsors, and the extent to which needs are being met. In benefiting from such a study, it may be possible to develop a more effective program with the available resources.

2. THREE ASPECTS OF LABOR TRAINING

In the past, the term "workers' education" has been applied to a number of differing educational efforts—vocational education, technical training, literacy or liberal-arts education, and trade-union training. While all of these do deal with education of workers, each is concerned with only a portion of the worker's life. Some of them are concerned with his employment, others with his personal life and well-being. Some presume that previous education and training were made available to the worker by his community, some are devoted to primary education.

The effectiveness and relevance of this education varies with the level of social and economic development in the worker's country and the traditions of his society. Thus, workers without any prior instruction must be taught basic literacy and the practical aspects of trade unionism, while those who have had some education and have taken active part in union work may be taught more advanced and theoretical aspects of labor-management relations and economic theory.

In considering the relevance of these forms of education and training to the problems of labor in developing nations, let us consider them in three categories: (1) literacy and general education; (2) the teaching of job or employment skills; and (3) the teaching of trade-union development skills.

Literacy is a necessity for wage earners if they are to perform anything more than basic unskilled manual labor. We in the United States seldom concern ourselves with literacy because it is no longer a problem for our workers. Because of our free and compulsory public school system, people entering the labor force are assured not merely of literacy but of a certain

14

amount of higher general education as well. American trade unions concentrate on academic studies that attempt to provide the rank and file with intellectual skills denied them by insufficient formal public schooling or premature abandonment of such schooling. The demands of the wage system have generally pulled young men and women from the classrooms either before they have acquired as much education as they would like or while they are in the midst of their basic formal schooling. The desires of workers everywhere to augment their learning so as to improve their positions in society and to adapt more readily to their environment and community has led to the establishment of many academic courses for workers. These range from hour-long lectures in union meeting halls to semester-long university courses. Sponsorship of these courses was assumed initially by the trade unions themselves, either by providing them directly or by encouraging other groups or the government to run them. The programs have since expanded to make courses available at both public and private institutions throughout the country. The subject matter taught may vary from political science to the fine arts—a broad range of material offered not only to satisfy the diverse curricular demands of the students, but also so that the rank and file may have a better understanding of their environment and be able to exercise their greatest potential as active participants in the community.

Because of our involvement in this level of education, we tend to underestimate the importance of, and widespread need for, literacy training in developing countries—the prerequisite of the general education in which our trade unions are so active.

Literacy training is probably the form of education most widely demanded by workers in Africa, Asia, and, to some extent, Latin America. Its importance to the workers is obvious when one considers the lack of public school facilities for the population as a whole; the rural background of the many workers who have come to the cities solely because more employment is available there; and the poverty of these workers, which precludes access to any education that might be available for payment of fees. In addition, even in the countries that have begun programs of widespread free education, the programs are usually intended for the young. Wage earners are in an age group that either grew up before such education was provided or was forced to abandon formal education, if available, in order to earn their living as part of the labor force.

The demands of workers for such education reflect the universal clamor for education from all groups in developing societies. But education for this segment of the population has the additional attribute of being particularly important to job advancement, to the employers' operation, and to the community's desire for a growing industrial economy. Their demands are also of great urgency because the education sought is not provided by existing institutions. In a few cases, local communities do provide literacy training and general education for adults and newly urbanized families, but by and large the urban workers are beyond the framework of public education.

Trade unions in developing countries have assumed much of the burden of literacy training for the wage-earning adult. Their efforts are less ambitious than government programs aimed at universal literacy, yet they have the advantage of selectivity, of reaching those who have already made a personal commitment to participation in economic development by abandoning the traditional subsistence economy, choosing wage employment, and thus demonstrating their personal energy and drive. A literacy program for these people may be more immediately rewarding than one aimed at *universal* literacy, especially when one considers the extensive costs that the latter would entail. The trade-union member, once he attains literacy, almost surely becomes a candidate for inclusion in more advanced training programs directly aimed at meeting the skill needs of the nation.

Literacy programs sponsored by trade unions are found around the world. In Zanzibar, for instance, a course in English is offered at union headquarters to the wives and children of members. In Calcutta, a group of Worker Education Societies meets several times a week in the evenings to teach Hindi and/or English to Bengali-speaking union members. In Lagos, one union holds several classes each evening in literacy and general education.

When such literacy programs are sufficiently widespread to meet the needs of the uneducated trade unionists, then perhaps the focus can turn toward more general forms of education.

The second aspect of education and training of labor is the teaching of employment skills. It is widely acknowledged that developing nations suffer from an acute shortage of certain skills essential to industrialization. By and large, these nations have succeeded in educating a sufficiently large cadre of professional personnel to meet the initial demands of their new national life. Undoubtedly the prestige attached to new government positions and the emphasis on professional education will help to fill the increasing demand for such personnel, as the governmental and commercial sectors expand with industrialization.

At the other extreme are the unskilled manual workers who are still largely bound to a subsistence economy and who possess no unique skill that can be applied to economic development. These, of course, constitute the great majority of the population and stand to gain the greatest advantage from programs of economic and social development.

Between these two groups is a middle group that must be exploited if the developing nation is to have the necessary manpower for industrialization. In this middle range are teachers, surveyors, bricklayers, social workers, carpenters, plumbers, and others. Economic and social development depends on augmenting their skills and encouraging increased numbers to enter these fields. At present, skilled workers of this kind are in crucially short supply, because: (1) the large rural population has never been provided with the requisite training or even literacy for learning these skills; (2) the governmental education system has traditionally emphasized "three R's" education rather than technical training; (3) persons with the resources for education turned to prestige positions rather than those less dramatic but perhaps even more important ones; and (4) those who have sufficient education and ability to learn and use these needed skills refuse to, because of the stigma attached to such employment, in many cases preferring to be underemployed in the "status" sectors of society.

Many devices are used to fill the gap in this middle-level manpower range. Governments are developing technical-training institutes, private industry is intensifying its on-the-job training programs and expanding them to include non-employees, and foreign governments and private groups are sending "Peace Corps" or the equivalent to meet short-term needs. Among these efforts are programs developed by the trade unions themselves. While it has been argued that skilled workers would be jealous of sharing their skills and would resist programs of instruction to newcomers, the traditions of apprenticeship, the overwhelming need for skilled workmen, and the evidence that skilled workers do support such programs belie this argument. Training of this sort was, in fact, organized by the early craft guilds during the embryonic era of trade unionism. Trade unions have also supported government technical-training programs in the public schools. In the United States, for instance, vocational training programs organized under the Smith-Hughes and George-Barden Acts train in those skills needed within the local community. Since the skills taught are among those widely organized by trade unions, the unions assist in administering the programs and introduce the student into wage employment through the apprenticeship system.

There are several examples of current trade-union sponsored vocational development programs in the new nations. In Algeria and Tunisia, the International Confederation of Free Trade Unions (ICFTU) has, through the Algerian Trade Union Federation (UGTA), organized vocational training courses in building and mechanical skills. Other countries have provided scholarships for workers to come to Germany, Austria, Switzerland, Israel, and elsewhere for training in manual and trade-union skills. An interesting program has been developed under the sponsorship of Israel's Histadrut and the Kenya Federation of Labor, teaching Kenyans not only construction skills but also the operation of consumer cooperatives. Another instance is in New York City, where the International Ladies' Garment Workers Union has a program for African trade unionists in job skills and union administration. Similarly, the Utility Workers of America, Local 1-2, has a program for technicians from Algeria, Morocco, Kenya, Nigeria, and Tunisia.

While these programs are but a small effort when compared to the over-all need for skilled manpower, they are noteworthy for several reasons. First, they constitute a new approach in international trade-union activity. Never before has there been any such direct attempt by workers in one country to improve the skill and earning capacity of workers in another country. The efforts are a new departure from the often criticized general-education programs considered earlier.

Secondly, these programs indicate that there is room for the participation of nongovernmental organizations in manpower development. Although missionary organizations and employers have long been actively interested in technical development, it is an area that is increasingly thought of as the government's concern. The costs of such training are great, and the prospect of programs organized under trade-union auspices on a wide geographic front is therefore rather limited. Yet the fact that the ICFTU and several of its affiliated national centers have found it financially possible to begin activities in this important field at all indicates that it may be possible to expand these direct programs. Certainly they will never meet all the needs, but they may help to relieve the pressure. They may prove to be a valuable supplement to government programs, by substituting a nongovernmental person-to-person relation. In this way, they would avoid indebtedness to any particular donor nation and permit the trade unions to augment their members' skills without being beholden to their national government.

Finally, these programs are of obvious value in meeting the

demands for technical skills in the nation concerned. It is fair to conclude that trade-union programs for technical training will probably be expanded as resources become available and as the unions become aware of the practical contribution they can make, and of the enhanced acceptability they will enjoy as a result.

Through manual-skill programs, trade unions in the United States and other industrialized countries have made a very real contribution to the development of middle-level manpower in their own and other countries. As highlighted by the Arden House Conference on Improving Work Skills in 1955:

> Unions can play a vital part in raising the skill level of the population through their role in apprenticeship programs, through their influence in determining seniority provisions, and through the assistance they could provide schools and other agencies in strengthening vocational guidance services and training programs.

The third aspect of workers' education—trade-union skills—is probably the most important, for it forms a base for all other educational activities. Without a strong development program and effective union leadership, none of the foregoing educational benefits can accrue. A weak and ineffective union, with a powerless leadership and an undirected membership, can do little to stimulate or create educational programs.

Trade unions in the developing countries need qualified and trained leaders—for administration of the union, for research, and for training of the rank and file. The last need is created by the lack of teaching personnel and school facilities, and by the need to overcome illiteracy and ignorance—the greatest handicaps to effective advancement of the trade unions and their members. Only through developing the leadership will it be possible to reach the rank and file, for educational resources are at present grossly inadequate for a direct program of rank-and-file education.

Leadership training will help the officials and potential leaders of the union to know and defend their legal rights and to discharge their responsibilities as workers and union members. Courses taught on subjects such as union administration, techniques of negotiation, labor laws, wage determination, effective communication with members, and on management, the public and the government, will help to achieve these goals.

The need for such courses reflects the even greater need to stimulate the rank and file in any organization to assume positions of leadership and to build unions that will protect and perpetuate democratic ideals in the trade-union movements of the free world. In this context, workers' education has one essential objective: to encourage potential leaders actively to participate in the functioning of the union and, thereby, to give members the knowledge and experience necessary for taking part in democratic political life.

Let us consider this objective in greater detail. Trade-union or labor education is intended to provide the workers of all nations and particularly of developing countries with a general understanding of their role in society and of their environment. It also seeks to provide them with some of the intellectual ammunition needed to assert their economic rights—through claims for higher wages, lower hours, better working conditions, and protection against the arbitrary actions of employers. This has been the lesson learned through practical experience of Western trade unionists. It is also the lesson now taught through formal education to less trained trade unionists in Asia, Africa, and Latin America.

As the sponsors of the Indian Government's Worker Education Scheme noted:

> In any democracy, the effectiveness of individual participation is ordinarily conditioned by the strength of the organization through which he has of necessity to function. The organization catering for workers in a democracy is their trade union. If industrial workers are to play their role properly in the affairs of the country, they should have strong, well organized and well informed trade unions run on constructive and responsible lines in the interest of the workers and of the country at large.

Leadership training programs are, then, desirable for all parts of society: for the worker, because it brings him an understanding of his proper role in the union and the economy, and of his legal and moral rights as an individual in asserting his demands; for the morally responsible citizen outside the union movement, who seeks to accord to each member of society not only a higher degree of education and training but also a fuller knowledge of his rights under democratic institutions; and even for the employers, who will profit from a responsible trade-union membership. Although it can be argued that strengthening the workers and the trade unions will severely handicap the accumulation and expansion of the capital necessary for economic development, the fact remains that no employer can expand his capital or introduce new equipment without a skilled labor force to perform the work.

In Africa at least, the development of a skilled labor force is handicapped by the absence of stability among the wage earners. Trade unions can contribute much toward the stability necessary to justify the employers' investment in training of unskilled workers for more advanced jobs. And trade unions generally provide a needed channel of communication between management and workers, making the employer-employee relationship one of truer mutual understanding.

Although governmental relations with trade unions in developing countries is acknowledged to create some problems, it is nevertheless true that unions have been in the vanguard in arousing public support for independence. Similarly, they can prove to be catalysts of economic development and political stability if the government recognizes them as autonomous partners in the effort. Further, the moral responsibility of the government for the improvement of the health and welfare to its citizens justifies support of programs that will ensure a higher standard of living.

There are two important aspects to trade-union training. The first is in leadership training and the second is in providing a practical demonstration of democracy and free institutions. As for the first problem, leadership training, it is widely recognized that one of the skills in shortest supply in developing countries is subprofessional administrative skill. This is important, whether it is practiced on behalf of an employer, the government or a union, because it encompasses discipline, group coordination, and the unity of purpose and effort so necessary in an industrializing society. It is perhaps most important in the unions, for in new nations, labor leaders often move on to government and managerial positions where their leadership training will prove to have been of the utmost importance.

In the area of functional or practical training in democratic procedures and techniques, it is obvious that trade unions are one of the most important, if not *the* most important, institution open to untrained and uneducated individuals where they can learn about and experience democracy. In many areas of the world, governments function from the top, with little or no participation by the individual even in choosing that government. Trade unions, cooperatives, youth groups, and the like are, then, the only structures acceptable to the entire community that have identified themselves with a pluralistic society. They can provide the populace with some degree of training, education, and experience in that self-expression and democratic organization which we in the West advocate throughout the world, and which, despite our outcries against oppression and our championing of democracy, has had little impact on those very people who should partake of it. The majority of people in Asia, Africa, and Latin America are still unaware of democracy except perhaps as a slogan of Western ideology. The severest handicap we face—particularly in Africa, where tribal structures bear greater resemblance to a communal way of life than to the individualistic—is our inability to bring democracy to the people who have, in the end, most to gain from it.

Trade unions are an accepted institution in modern society and a leading organized group in national life. They function beyond the narrow confines of local demands for improvement in wages, hours, and working conditions, and assume broad social, economic, and even political responsibilities. Accordingly, trade unions are a potentially valuable vehicle for putting across our democratic ideas at the level of society where they are most needed, and where they may some day have a profound effect on the political futures of new nations. There is some evidence that this system of grass-roots education has already been effective, or has, at least, made men who would otherwise be passive think and even act about their right to protest. Perhaps trade-union training will have a more rapid and more valuable impact in the new nations than the costly, long-term, universal primary education now so highly recommended. It seems reasonable to expect that workers exposed to such training would be less willing to surrender their rights to totalitarian governments.

The question naturally arises as to how one is to teach these principles of democracy. Can we in the West provide some of the techniques of democracy that will enable these new nations to develop their own political institutions in a democratic framework?

Trade unions, cooperatives, youth groups, and the other voluntary institutions that proliferate in our own society do have valuable lessons to impart to similar groups in developing nations. Although the techniques of training leaders must be considerably altered and adapted to have any impact abroad, the very existence of the organizations is important. For the education offered by these institutions to develop leaders not only meets the immediate economic and political demands for leadership, but, more important, stimulates the growth of the institutions themselves.

In the United States, we all too often overlook the valuable contribution to our own development made by trade unions. When we are confronted with the confusion created by strikes, emergency disputes, racketeering investigations, and the like, our forgetfulness is easy to understand. Yet the American trade-union movement developed as a generally peaceful, non-violent, nonpolitical institution. It has in recent years obtained increased benefits through peaceful negotiations and lobbying through existing political parties. It has abided by the framework of American democracy and geared its actions to improving its economic position by using the facilities provided by existing social institutions. In Europe, one sees a multitude of labor-supported political parties, labor legislation confiscating private property, governments overthrown, and public strikes in support of political objectives. Our trade-union movement has developed in the context of wide-open spaces, equal opportunity, freedom of expression, and vertical mobility, all of which have led the unions to consider themselves as peaceful representatives of labor in dealing with employers on matters confined to wages, hours, and working conditions. The frequent failure of early American labor parties and their continuing inability to "deliver the labor vote" or impress upon the dues-paying union members a sense of a labor interest that surmounts sectional, entrepreneurial, veteran, or other personal interests testify to the extent to which our trade-union tradition may hopefully be of some assistance in bringing ultimate political stability to the troubled countries of Africa, Asia, and Latin America. The inheritance of Continental trade-union structures in most developing countries accounts for an understandable fear on the part of new political leaders that a free and uncontrolled trade-union movement may, at present, inspire economic and political opposition to government development plans, which, in turn, might encourage a vociferous political opposition and lead to the downfall of incumbent politicians. Such reasoning obscures, however, the long-term benefits obtained from democratic trade-union movements.

The several aspects of workers' education considered in this chapter will constitute the basis for examining the international efforts being made to meet the needs for union leadership in Africa, Asia, and Latin America.

3. TRAINING FOR LABOR LEADERSHIP

Trade-union leadership training does not come neatly wrapped in a prepared package. Varying with the specific needs of the sponsors, students, and trade unions involved, several different approaches have been used in the world-wide effort to stimulate trade-union development. But, in each case, the sponsor has shown a recognition of the immediacy of the need and a desire to achieve the best results in the shortest time, using the available and usually limited resources. Various programs continue to function simultaneously but generally without contact with others of the same sort. Although greater coordination would be desirable, there is no denying that nearly every effort in the field of labor leadership training is of real value.

The catalog of current leadership training activities includes programs of visits to industrialized nations, as well as short-term classroom courses and longer resident training courses, in both industrialized and developing nations. Probably the most publicized of these is the so-called leader grant. Under such a grant, a trade unionist is provided with a comprehensive tour in one of the more industrialized countries, usually in Western Europe or North America. The sponsor expects that he will learn the techniques and accomplishments of more highly developed trade unions and return with sufficient direction and enthusiasm to steer his own union along new paths.

These grants have undoubtedly been successful in showing to their recipients the customs, habits, and institutions of the industrialized countries, also in establishing closer political ties between union leaders in America or Europe and in the emerging states. But they have not been noted for success in teaching trade-union development, for several reasons. In the first place, the selection of participants is not always based entirely on merit. The selection procedure remains largely in the hands of officials of the sponsoring organization or government of the country to which the visitor comes, although his own government also may exercise a controlling voice for its own political purposes. Those officials do not necessarily select the trade unionists with the greatest potential for contributing to union development. Actually, the devoted trade unionist is likely to be too deeply involved in his work to be willing to absent himself for an extended period of time. The sponsor of the leader grant is likely to select a politically oriented trade unionist, usually one with facility in English, French, or Spanish, who has made his presence, as well as his willingness to see the sponsor's country, known. Sometimes he is the type who manifests a cynical or dubious attitude toward his prospective host simply for the purpose of stimulating an invitation. Usually, he is one who can be spared from the day-to-day union operations for the length of a visit. As a result, he is often a "second stringer." Although the receiving of a leader grant is a desirable status symbol for many, in several countries it has come to be viewed by the rank and file as evidence of "selling out" to the bribes of a foreign government.

Secondly, the visits are generally too short to permit any realistic program of trade-union study. Although some grants do permit up to a year of study, the average last from three to twelve weeks. During this period, the grantee is whisked from place to place in what usually amounts to little more than a sightseeing tour. He has little opportunity to get the feel of a community, much less learn any lessons in trade unionism.

In addition, the itinerary generally reflects the visitor's personal desires rather than any concerted program of trade-union orientation. This is further complicated when the host government wishes him to see the breadth and scope of the country and visit certain prestige spots; the visitor has time for little more than a rubbernecking tour with occasional quick calls upon local unions en route. The officials who make out the itinerary are aware of this danger but are usually reluctant to insist on a particular stop or series of visits for fear that it would antagonize the visitor and destroy the value of the whole exercise.

Finally, even in those nations that provide grants with an opportunity for formal training, the union leader from the developing country is usually put in a class of students of the host country (or, at best, an international class of trade unionists from several countries) where most of what is taught is either too general or too advanced to be of much practical value, and where there is a strong tendency to focus primarily on trade-union practices in the host country itself. It is reasonable to conclude that, due to his lack of exposure to the country's customs, institutions, and practices, the participant will profit little from enrollment in such courses. The disparity of cultural background generally prevents him from absorbing the full impact of the lessons. It is as if a graduate seminar were opened to primary and secondary school students. If he learns anything, it is likely to be irrelevant to the real purpose —for example, the comparative affluence of the local union officials. (This has backfired on more than one occasion, when the grantee returned home to use improper methods to achieve that affluence.) Despite these difficulties, the leader-grant programs, administered by governments of the industrialized countries, continue to attract trade unionists from Africa, Asia, and Latin America.

Similar programs undertaken by the trade unions of industrialized countries without government sponsorship face the same problems. In many instances, the programs continue nevertheless, particularly in Europe, but there is a growing feeling that more effective work can be done on the spot, in the developing nations of the world. Thus, there has been a shift to programs carried out in the context of the developing trade unions themselves, particularly in the formal education programs, where classes that mix trade unionists from advanced and less developed countries can be avoided. While there is a great deal to be gained from comparative studies of trade-union development, it is far more valuable to present a course specifically concerned with the unique problems of one trade-union structure, when all the participants share the same background and traditions.

This trend toward indigenous training of trade-union leaders seems to be a more realistic approach to imparting practical techniques of trade-union development. But, while many governments have endorsed such programs, the leader grants continue for their political if not for their educational value. Classroom education in trade-union development is being carried on at many levels in Africa, Asia, and Latin America. It has even been carried out by assigning experienced trade unionists from industrialized countries to work as advisors to the trade unions in developing countries. Day-long, weekend, week, or month-long courses are tailored to teach a specific subject or group of subjects to a specific group of unionists. In the free world, such courses are organized on local, national, and regional bases by national centers, the International Confederation of Free Trade Unions (ICFTU), the International Federation of Christian Trade Unions (IFCTU), the International Trade Secretariats (ITS), and the International Labor Organization (ILO). Their effectiveness is undoubtedly greater than leader-grant programs, if only because of the greater number of union members involved, the excessive transportation costs avoided, and the specifically tailored curriculums. An attempt to catalog fully all such activities and their sponsors would be not only futile but most likely incomplete.

Probably the most ambitious and most striking of the on-the-spot educational projects are those that were planned as resident training institutions offering a full curriculum of trade-union training over an extended period, usually three or four months. In addition to their greater educational value, the centers are also important because they act as a permanent focus for trade-union activity in the region and also perform the duties of a clearing-house and advisory group on new techniques in trade-union development. These centers are a most promising innovation in labor training. They have been developed by a variety of sponsors for a variety of purposes. Their structure, selection techniques, curriculums, teaching techniques, and impact differ, yet they have in common a single purpose of providing needed instruction to a certain segment of society. The sponsors feel that this instruction is essential not only to the trade unionists themselves, but to the community in which they live.

4. NINE RESIDENT LABOR TRAINING CENTERS

There are at present a multitude of resident labor training centers throughout the world. Trade unions in the industrialized nations have long relied on such centers for development of trade-union leadership, but only in the last decade have they appeared in Africa, Asia, and Latin America. In some cases, these centers are national ones, geared to meet the specific needs of a single nation. In other cases, they have been developed by an international organization, bringing together trade unionists from a certain region or group of countries for training. Some are sponsored by governments, some by trade unions, some by both. The following brief descriptions of nine such centers is arranged chronologically in the order of their creation. A detailed description of each may be found in the appendixes.

Labor Relations Institute of the University of Puerto Rico

The Institute began its first international program in 1951 in cooperation with ORIT, the American regional organization of the ICFTU. There were six Latin American labor leaders in this first course, which lasted for seventeen weeks. ORIT financed the transportation, the University provided for them while they were in Puerto Rico, and the U.S. Government offered a two-month tour of the United States following completion of the course. In 1953, ORIT ended its formal relationship with the Institute, but subsequent U.S. Government technical assistance programs continued the selection and financing of participants. Courses are held three times a year with a maximum enrollment of twenty-five students; to date, more than 650 Spanish-speaking trade unionists from twenty-two countries have participated. The Institute also trains Puerto Rican union officials at a resident training center at the University and in extension courses held throughout the island, a program financed with regular University funds.

The Institute's latest program was inaugurated early in 1962, in cooperation with the New York State School of Industrial and Labor Relations at Cornell University, exclusively for the training of labor educators from Latin America. This course is limited to students from a single industry or group of industries. The program functions in close cooperation with the ITS of the industry concerned and is financed by a grant from the Marshall Foundation.

The selection of participants in the original ORIT program was left largely in the hands of ORIT itself. In subsequent programs, the U.S. Government agency concerned became involved in the selection procedure. The nominations for participants made by unions and the labor ministries are subject to a veto by the U.S. Operations Missions. Final selection in the new Labor Educator program is carried on by the Institute itself, the ITS concerned, and the participating trade-union organization in the respective countries.

The Institute uses the services of the University of Puerto Rico faculty members, trade-union leaders, and U.S. Government labor officers to teach courses in union administration, labor legislation, economics, and negotiation. The same curriculum is used for both the national and international courses with different emphasis on uniquely Puerto Rican or generally Latin American problems. In the Labor Education program, the emphasis is on specialized techniques of labor education.

Most classes are group discussions, although there are occasional lectures. Field trips in Puerto Rico are used as well.

ICFTU Asian Trade-Union College, Calcutta

The International Confederation of Free Trade Unions was formed in 1949 by democratically oriented trade-union national centers. Using money contributed to its Regional Activitics Funds by its members, the ICFTU established a permanent school where officials from affiliated national unions in developing Asian countries could undertake concentrated studies in various aspects of trade-union development, Calcutta was chosen as the location for the first such school, which was opened on November 5, 1952.

The college is entirely financed and operated by the ICFTU. It offers courses for Indian and other union leaders, varying from weekend ones devoted to a particular local subject to three-month courses for union leaders of Burma, Republic of China, Ceylon, Hong Kong, Japan, Malaya, Okinawa, Pakistan, the Philippines, Singapore, and Thailand. Students are selected by national affiliates of the ICFTU and are financed by their own union, the ICFTU, or from their own personal funds. The subjects taught include economic theory and the analysis of democratic institutions, but the greatest emphasis is on practical aspects of union building—methods of dues collection, techniques of collective bargaining, processing of employee grievances, and the like. At first, teaching was done solely by lecture, but in recent years the Director of the school, V. S. Mathur, has developed a different system, whereby courses begin with assigned study guides and group discussion followed by an occasional lecture.

The college has also established a unique system of worker-education centers that cater to the diversified needs of the rank and file. It has also held many refresher courses for former students combined with field courses in the several national centers of Asia. As of March, 1963, 21 international courses for 562 Asian students, and 16 Indian courses for 341 students had been held at the college, as well as more than 65 short courses and seminars in a dozen other countries for 2017 participants.

Labor Education Center of the University of the Philippines

This center was established as a joint project of the U.S. Foreign Operations Administration and the Philippine National Economic Council in 1952. After initial efforts to stimulate union growth through the Philippine trade unions directly, it was agreed to establish a formal Labor Education Center to be administered by the University of the Philippines. In May, 1954, the new center was inaugurated as a joint ICA-NEC project. From then until 1962, the program was directed by Dr. Cicero Calderon. The program, originally intended to stimulate trade-union development throughout the Philippines, operated out of headquarters in Manila, with permanent field offices in Luzon, Visayas, and Mindanao. U.S. Government sponsorship continued until 1958, when total financing and sponsorship shifted to the Government of the Philippines. Since then, the domestic program has continued to expand without U.S. participation, and a new Asian program for foreign union leaders has been inaugurated with renewed U.S. Government support.

The domestic program includes weekend institutes in the field for the rank and file; training programs for union officials, at locations throughout the islands; Union Education Directors' Institutes; Trade-Union Research Institutes; non-labor seminars for public school teachers, police officers, and management; and a resident training school with courses in advanced techniques of trade unionism, open to graduates of the basic local courses. By 1962, 385 such institutes and courses had been held with a total attendance exceeding 15,000.

In addition to the formal courses, the Center has developed a noteworthy program with audio-visual aids and its substantial library.

Students are selected either from the rank and file for introductory courses or from among trade-union leaders for advanced courses. Their attendance is financed by their trade unions.

The curriculum is a practical one, stressing trade-union development in the context of economic development. Since the program is national, particular emphasis is placed on utilizing available government facilities and legislation to attain trade-union goals. The courses are largely organized in lectures, followed by discussion groups, although it is likely that there will be greater reliance on audio-visual facilities in the future.

In January, 1960, the Center began a new program for trade-union officials from other Asian countries. It is financed jointly by U.S. Government technical-assistance funds and the University of the Philippines, with scholarship aid coming from ILO, UNESCO, and the Asia Foundation. Students from Burma, Ceylon, China, Hong Kong, India, Indonesia, Japan, Korea, Malaya, Pakistan, and the Philippines have attended the course, which lasts for ten weeks. Selection of the participants is made by the U.S. Operations Missions and the national trade-union centers or ministries of labor. The courses were originally conducted only in English, but simultaneous translations have been recently introduced. The content of these courses is naturally more international and probably more academic than the domestic Philippine program. They stress trade unions and democracy, union structure, social legislation, contemporary labor problems in participating countries, and the techniques of labor education. More than 125 students completed the international course in its first two years; some of them were instrumental in establishing similar domestic programs, on their own or with government support, in their own countries.

ICFTU African Labor College, Kampala

The ICFTU's satisfaction with the progress of its Asian College in Calcutta led it to open a second resident training center in Kampala, Uganda, in 1958, for trade-union leaders from affiliated English-speaking national unions in Africa.

The college conducts a four-month resident course, as well as field courses in other countries taught by Kampala staff members and alumni. It has also established a research center in Kampala to compile statistical data in labor relations, greatly needed by economists in Africa. In 1963, it inaugurated an intensive and specialized resident course in labor education, research, and union administration. Students are selected from nominations made by participating national centers, and have come from Aden, Cameroon, Ethiopia, Gambia, Ghana, Kenya, Liberia, Libya, Mauritius, Nigeria, Northern Rhodesia, Nyasaland, Sierra Leone, Somalia, Southern Rhodesia, Tanganyika, Uganda, and Zanzibar. There have been seven courses held, with 259 participants.

Emphasis has shifted from lectures to discussion groups on foreign trade-union movements; trade-union structure and administration; particular trade-union, economic, and social problems in Africa; labor laws and legislation; and techniques of communication and workers' education. The success of the Kampala operations has led the ICFTU to initiate a college for French-speaking African trade unionists in West Africa.

Indian Government Workers' Education Scheme

In 1958, the Indian Ministry of Labor and Employment, in cooperation with four national trade unions, universities, and employer associations, established the Central Board for Workers' Education. This Board was created to operate an educational program for trade-union leaders and, more important, for the rank and file. The program is arranged on three levels. At the highest level are the Education Officers, who are selected from the academic community as well as from national trade unions. They are given six months of intensive training in academic and practical subjects, with emphasis on the techniques of workers' education. The union members of this group are then encouraged to return to their unions and establish educational programs, for which government financial assistance is available. Those taken from the academic community are assigned to one of the fourteen regional centers established throughout the country to train at the second level of the structure—the Worker-Teachers. The students at this level are selected from the working force of participating companies. The courses last for three months, after which the Worker-Teachers return to their employment and teach the rank and file on the third level. This is done in their place of employment and usually for an hour or so a day, frequently on company time.

The program is financed entirely by the Indian Government, except that Worker-Teachers are compensated by their employer during their training and receive an extra stipend for teaching the rank and file in their companies. More than 2,500 Worker-Teachers and over 46,000 rank-and-file workers had completed such training by March, 1963.

The curriculum is more general than any of the others in international worker-education programs, for the greatest emphasis is placed on the role of trade unions and workers in building the economy of India. Little, if any, emphasis is placed on the techniques of building strong independent trade unions. There is, of course, no teaching of strike techniques and the like, primarily because the program is oriented toward gaining mass support for the government's development program. Lectures are used extensively, but there is time devoted each day to group discussions.

Histadrut's Afro-Asian Labor Institute, Tel Aviv

Histadrut, the General Federation of Jewish Labor in Israel, has for several years brought union leaders from Asia and Africa to Israel for special training. In 1960, it launched its Afro-Asian Institute as a permanent resident program for trade-union leaders from the underdeveloped nations of Asia and Africa. The program is financed by Histadrut, which is a labor, employer, and quasi-official government complex. The

AFL-CIO and British TUC provide support in the form of scholarship funds to match Israeli contributions. Begun as a school for trade-union leaders as well as administrators of cooperatives, it modified its structure after the first course to train the trade unionists in a separate program. Students or their sponsors must arrange for the cost of transportation and family subsistence, but some scholarship funds are available. As many as seventy unionists, half French-speaking and half English-speaking, are taught separately in four-month courses that include formal classroom lectures in French or English without translators. In addition, there are sessions with tutors and extensive field trips, which include assignments in fields of their interest at Israeli plants and trade unions.

The students are usually nominated by Israeli embassy officials in the various countries, but many students have applied to the Institute directly or through their national trade union. Students have attended from Basutoland, Burma, the Central African Republic, Ceylon, Chad, the Congos (Brazzaville and Leopoldville), Cyprus, Dahomey, Ethiopia, Gambia, Ghana, India, Iran, Ivory Coast, Japan, Kenya, Liberia, Malagasy, Malaya, Mali, Nepal, Nigeria, Nyasaland, the Philippines, Northern and Southern Rhodesia, Senegal, Sierra Leone, Singapore, South Africa, Surinam, Swaziland, Tanganyika, Thailand, Togo, Uganda, Upper Volta, and Zanzibar. The curriculum covers cooperation, labor economics and economic development. The emphasis is on cooperation with other segments of society; comparatively little time is devoted to the skills of building trade unions as a power force in the country.

ICFTU Inter-American Residential Institute for Labor Studies, Mexico City

On April 2, 1962, ORIT opened a Residential Institute for Labor Studies in Mexico, with the initial aim of training teachers, and a subsequent objective of training organizers, youth leaders, labor journalists, and researchers. In its first three courses, it trained 110 such students.

Students are nominated by affiliated national trade-union centers, hopefully from among those who have already attended local ORIT seminars. ORIT finances their attendance, with the understanding that the national centers will use them as labor educators upon their return.

The course of study places greatest emphasis on techniques of establishing and running worker-education programs, but also devotes some attention to substantive political, social, and economic problems confronting trade unions in Latin America. Most subjects are discussed in small group meetings after a brief introductory lecture. The course concludes with a panel discussion of the findings of the study groups. Students of the second course visited Israel as the guests of Histadrut for five weeks in October, 1962, on completion of their studies.

According to reports from students in the first course, 80 per cent were active in educational programs within six months of their return home.

American Institute for Free Labor Development, Washington

Following the experience of the Post, Telegraph, and Telecommunications International Secretariat (PTTI) in running a training course for Latin Americans at Front Royal, Virginia, the AFL-CIO was instrumental in establishing the American Institute for Free Labor Development, with headquarters in Washington. This Institute was formally launched on May 29, 1962, with a Board of Directors composed of union officials and U.S. and Latin American businessmen. Carrying out its initial activities with the assistance of a $250,000 grant from the U.S. Agency for International Development, the Institute anticipates that future programs will be sustained by foundation contributions.

As in the case of other training programs, the Institute offers a three-month training course in the techniques of union development. The fundamental difference between this and other courses is that participants here return to their respective union movements with a specific commitment to organize the unorganized. To facilitate their efforts and to remove them from the day-to-day problems of union administration, the Institute provides a nine-month salary subsidy when they have finished the course. The sponsors hope that the trained trade unionist will build up his union's strength so that it will be self-sufficient and no longer in need of external subsidization.

The first course given by the Institute ran from June 18 to September 14, 1962, and was divided into two class groups— one in English and one in Spanish. It is anticipated that there will be 100–120 Latin American trade unions joining the program each year. Regional and national training centers are being established to facilitate the Institute's activities, and social projects departments are anticipated in the various Latin American countries.

The curriculum of the course includes training in the skills of trade-union development, such as collective bargaining and contract administration, and also concepts of the trade union as an essential element in democracy, and techniques of fighting Communist and fascist infiltration.

International Institute for Labor Studies, Geneva

The International Labor Organization, long a contributor to the development of democratic trade unionism, announced its entry into the field of labor education on March 1, 1960. Its International Institute for Labor Studies, which held its first course from September 17 to December 7, 1962, is not a labor training center like the other ones considered here. Rather, it is a center for advanced studies for professionals in labor, management and the government where they can come for three months of specialized training in labor-management relations, absorb some of the wealth of experience of the officials and staff of the ILO, and improve their perspective on other sectors by constant exposure and group living with labor, management, and government officials.

The Institute is administered independently of the ILO, although its staff and board are chosen through ILO procedures. It will be financed by an independent $10,000,000 endowment, which will provide an operating budget of approximately $300,000. Participants can apply to attend the program either as individuals or as representatives of a labor, management, or government organization. Preference is given to applicants with such sponsorship. No more than one student is selected from each country, but there is no attempt to regulate the percentage of labor, management, or government officials taking part. (Thirty individuals were selected to participate in the first course and twenty-nine took part: twelve from government, twelve from labor, and five from management.) A university education is preferred and the majority of participants had had graduate training, although several had only secondary school educations. Most of the students are from Africa and Asia, although there are some from Europe and the Western Hemisphere.

The curriculum is a highly specialized and comparative one. It emphasizes advanced concepts of the role and problems of labor in the emerging nations of the world. The course is composed primarily of lectures, with daily opportunity for reading and discussion of the lectures. One or two lectures a day are offered in simultaneous translation; the discussions are held in three groups—two English-speaking and one French-speaking.

This brief catalog of existing programs gives an idea of their geographical spread, as well as of their internal operations. A detailed study of each would no doubt lead to the conclusion that each has made a significant contribution to developing the techniques of trade-union training. But such a study would not be likely to reveal the fundamental contrasts and problems inherent in government vs. trade-union operation, national vs. international programs, etc.

It is necessary to point out the particular strengths or weaknesses of one approach in contrast to another in a given area, and to study the basic philosophical and practical problems arising in the different centers.

5. OBJECTIVES OF THE SPONSORS

Despite the general view that labor training is desirable and should be encouraged and expanded, it is clear that individual centers for such training and the sponsors of them consider the training as important from their own perspective and in line with the unique needs of their own community. Accordingly, the sponsor's motivation is of utmost importance, particularly when the students of the centers come from backgrounds of limited education and are likely to accept the lessons offered as unchallengeable guides to their own futures. The limited number of labor training centers, in contrast to the great number of people wanting to gain admission, makes it likely that one person will be able to attend only one such center. He will be unable to gain a clear perspective on the center's orientation and will probably accept what is taught as the gospel truth.

It is, of course, impossible to prescribe what the orientation should be in every training center; indeed, to be able to do so would imply that freedom of self-determination and choice in the matter were lacking. Nonetheless, it is valuable to look at the various approaches used in the programs, with the aim of developing a view as to what the ideal orientation should be. Does the course meet only the sponsor's needs or does it seek to benefit the working community or society as a whole? In the answer to this question lies the foundation for the development or strengthening of labor training programs.

Each party concerned in union training undoubtedly has a different objective in view. The rank-and-file union member views such training, in theory at least, as an opportunity to gain the practical information that will make him a better

43

organizer, negotiator, administrator, or labor educator, so that he can improve the standard of living of his fellow union members. Most trade unionists also view such training as an opportunity for personal advancement. Education and travel abroad, new status symbols in the developing nations, will inevitably place the participant in a position where he can advance his personal career through the trade union, or through employment by management or in the government.

At present, trade-union officials, as distinguished from the rank and file, view labor training programs either as means for training new leaders in techniques of improving the workers' conditions, or more negatively, as a means for training those young leaders in techniques that may ultimately pose a threat to their own power. If the officials possess the devotion to their unions indicated by the first view, then they will send their brightest aides or local officials, to strengthen the ranks of leadership or to train successors—usually at considerable personal sacrifice, since they will have to continue without assistance during the duration of the course. If, on the other hand, the trade-union official views the training as a threat to his position, he may send the "second stringer" or the unionist to whom he owes a political or personal debt—as a means of "pay-off" and as a protection against the loss of his own power.

The government viewpoint in the emerging nations naturally varies from country to country. In nations with a strong drive toward economic development, a dynamic trade-union movement is viewed as a threat to the accumulation of private or public capital (particularly in countries with a large government sector), as a force that should be steered toward supporting and contributing to government development plans, rather than one that should be encouraged to fight freely for the rights of its members. This attitude has been taken at those centers where the labor training is geared to the concept of labor-management-government cooperation in building the country. In more than one country, the government has established its own training program to emphasize the importance of full support for its development plans. This perforce minimizes the workers' exposure to such essential and legitimate trade-union lessons as dues collection, effective negotiation, and strike techniques.

Some of these same nations, particularly those in Africa and Latin America, view labor training programs as a political as well as an economic threat and are reluctant to allow unionists to learn the lessons that might make them politically powerful. They fear that unionists will learn the techniques of communication and leadership that will enable them effectively to oppose the government or undermine its popular support and thus develop in opposition to the government.

Other nations, either because their government is more strongly oriented to labor or because of more deeply entrenched democratic traditions, encourage programs in trade-union development as an effective way of carrying to the people the essential lessons of self-government and functional democracy, or as the best means of offering a fundamental education to the rank and file. Finally, they may consider the programs as a valuable means for teaching democratic ideals, problems in social economics, and administrative techniques to future economic and political leaders.

When certain nations are willing or eager to serve as hosts or organizers of international labor training programs, it is evident that their motivation goes beyond that of a government seeking merely to stimulate its own trade-union movement. That motivation is probably more political than social or economic: It depends on a desire to spread understanding of the nation's activities by exposing foreign trade unionists to its philosophy and ideology. There may also be a desire for economic or political prestige—a desire to gain understanding among the future political and economic leaders of the emerging countries.

The United States Government seems to approve of the programs undertaken by the trade unions themselves, for it avoids the dangers of governmental controls. It acknowledges that worker education really falls within the trade unions' exclusive jurisdiction. However, it recognizes the great financial burdens of administering such programs and is willing to infringe on the unions' prerogatives in order to cooperate with them in joint efforts whenever possible. Such activities are not foreign to a government that has long supported general education, skill development, and apprenticeship training, that so dynamically stimulated workers' education by establishing the land-grant college system. The U.S. Government appears to have achieved rapport with the American trade-union movement in this field because of similarity in objectives and ideals. Cooperation can, of course, only succeed when there is this identity of purpose and when the unions are willing to have a government take part in what are legitimately union activities. The U.S. Government seems to be more often in agreement with the American union movement than are governments of other countries with theirs. This obviously raises great problems, because in trade-union training programs in developing countries, the U.S. Government must necessarily work through representatives of the foreign governments. If the foreign government actively discourages or only barely tolerates the development of independent trade unions, then there are bound to be problems in the rapport with or support for American activities in this field. It should also be noted that the United States does not act entirely altruistically in this field. It feels a genuine need to stimulate democratic institutions in the newly developing states, and not only for the benefits that such programs bring to the union members; it also seeks to perpetuate and encourage the very concept of democracy inherent in self-governing institutions of a stable society, the concept that is presumed to be our great strength and our contribution to the development of the free world.

A few words should also be added about the attitude of American trade unions toward programs of trade-union leadership development. It is obvious from AFL-CIO support of the ICFTU's Solidarity Fund, of the Institute for Free Labor Development, and of various national trade-union centers, that American labor supports and encourages education in democratic trade unionism through such training programs. This effort identifies its goal with the government's—that of seeking to stimulate democratic ideals. On occasion, it has had difficulty when it finds the government of the United States, or of any other country, participating in internal trade-union affairs. Even though the participation may be constructive and may help to achieve the union's own long-range goals, American labor's tradition of independence of, and separation from, government logically results in calling such government activity interference. This viewpoint is intensified by the obvious desire of certain foreign governments to minimize effective unionization or to curtail strikes as a price for participation in training programs, if the foreign governments are to remain loyal to their own objectives of stimulating economic development and political unity. The recent evidence of cooperation between the AFL-CIO and the Agency for International Development in sponsoring the American Institute for Free Labor Development indicates that there is a possibility for cooperation, provided that the aims of the participants are similar and that the administration of the program includes trade unions as an equal or controlling partner.

The varying motivations behind trade-union and governmental support of labor training programs indicate the difficulty of planning a program that will satisfy all demands. But when the demands are for personal glorification and advancement, they do not warrant satisfaction, unless the sponsors wish nothing more than to win friends on a superficial political basis. Obviously, that is not the legitimate goal of labor training programs.

But on a more serious level, there are certain fundamental differences in objectives that do have a direct bearing on development of labor training programs. There are those who seek to use trade-union training to stimulate economic development and at the same time attempt to restrict those aspects of it that might create economic or political unrest, stimulate potential political opposition, or deprive employers (both public and private) of profits available for reinvestment. There are also those who seek to stimulate independent and democratic trade unions in new nations regardless of the effect on development plans.

Although these arguments might appear to be merely issues of curriculum or methodology, they are more than that, for they concern the very sponsorship and structure of labor training programs. Several types of programs are feasible.

The first is a government program intended to incorporate the trade unions as a tool in economic development, providing trade unionists with an education that would intensify their desire to assist in the building of a new nation without regard to personal wishes or comfort and with a willingness to forego personal rights and benefits. The emphasis would be on general education and on the structure of political and economic institutions, rather than on the roles of trade unions as the democratic voices of the workers, collective bargainers, strike organizers, or grievance supporters. Information on protective legislation might also be suppressed if it were felt that a workers's assertion of his rights might jeopardize the country's development plans. Fortunately none of the existing programs in the free world shows such motivation or uses such methods. It is obvious that this approach would, within a short time, eradicate from the worker's mind the ideal of independent trade unionism and would undoubtedly destroy the program's vitality, particularly if the union leadership were captured by the political powers and there were no opportunity for the workers to gain an understanding of how free trade unions can or should function.

At the other extreme is the program sponsored strictly by the trade union, which, in teaching the lessons of free and democratic trade unions, might create a dissident force capable of destroying all government efforts to achieve a viable economy or polity. Such a program might also discourage private investment, and even public investment, by reducing the prospects of earning a return sufficient to justify the further investment in new fields that is so essential for developing the economy. This action could prove even more disastrous if the unions encouraged political activity on the part of their leaders. Fortunately, this extreme has also failed to materialize, and the trade-union programs and their supporters find that the primary problem is not in the danger of an unscrupulous trade union acting irresponsibly, but, rather, in the lack of finances needed to continue to expand the responsible job they have done so far. Most observers acknowledge that trade-union programs of workers' education are the most desirable, but a trade-union program free of government interference or control must be financed solely by the trade unions. Union members in industrialized countries are preoccupied with their own domestic problems and unfortunately are not sufficiently oriented to the needs of their untrained fellow workers in Asia, Africa, and Latin America to support adequately the needed programs. As a result, trade-union training programs remain but a drop in the bucket, in terms of their actually meeting the needs of the workers and of democratic governments in the less developed nations of the world.

Between the extremes of government subversion of free trade unions on the one hand, and the trade unions' inability to finance needed programs on the other, a meeting ground of cooperation between governments and trade unions must be found if the largest possible number of workers are to be taught the lessons of free trade unionism and democratic institution building. The present government programs encompass some of the possibilities—ranging from the Indian Government's program with active trade-union participation to trade-union programs that use government funds solely for transportation costs.

Trade union assistance from outside sources for workers' education seems to be acceptable only:

1. If the aims of the agency giving assistance are not in conflict with those of the trade union concerned.

2. If the agency offering assistance believes in, and stands for, democracy.

3. If the acceptance of assistance from the agency does not entail any obligation on the part of the receiving trade union

that might jeopardize its freedom of action and independence.

4. If the acceptance of such assistance has no influence on the contents of the programs conducted by the receiving trade union.

While the goals are not always completely achieved, they still define the cooperative relation between governments and trade unions.

In its Asian Conference on Trade Union Education of November 19–26, 1962, the ICFTU members accepted the possibility of assistance through travel grants, the supply of literature, equipment, and accommodations, and leave with or without pay to members to enable them to attend educational programs. It did, however, recommend against the acceptance of cash assistance.

The following chapters in this volume will compare various facets of existing programs, the implications of the several sponsorships, and their impact on the content of the courses.

6. PROBLEMS OF STRUCTURE

The ways in which sponsors of the various labor training centers have organized their programs and teaching efforts are quite diverse. Some of the programs have a national enrollment; others are international; still others alternate national with international courses. Some are centralized, holding their sessions in a single location, while others emphasize field classes; some of the courses run for only a few days, while others last up to six months. Some have only ten students, while others have as many as seventy. Some are taught by trade unionists, others by academicians. Running through all these variations is the constant problem of financing, and who is to do it.

International vs. National Programs

The rapid growth of labor training programs after World War II, coupled with the great number of different sponsors of such programs, resulted in a haphazard development of training centers throughout the world.

The early programs were initiated in only a few of the countries where the need was obvious and democratic trade-union teaching would have been acceptable. Subsequently, programs were planned in other countries to meet unfulfilled needs there, and expanded in the regions where programs already existed in order to serve the particular purposes of the new sponsors. As a result, there are now a number of both international and domestic programs, and more than one center serving each major geographical area. Is the international approach preferable to the domestic one? Should there be strict delineation of geographical jurisdiction among the sponsors or restrictions on the number of programs in a particular area? The development of both national and international programs in several continents provides an opportunity to examine the effectiveness of each approach.

International programs have several benefits. They bring together trade unionists from neighboring countries for a common sharing of experience, and permit the participants from more backward nations to profit from the experiences of their more advanced neighbors. They stimulate the camaraderie which is one of the keystones of trade unionism in the free world. At the same time, they permit a comparative study of local problems and a common attempt at their solution. Also, they provide a means by which one center can help to meet the needs of a multitude of countries without duplicating facilities and staff. They enable the trade unionist to leave his usual context of family and union, so that he may study without distraction and view the problems of his own country from a different perspective. Finally, in the cases where training is provided in a more advanced but still developing location— Israel or Puerto Rico—they permit a study of the progress enjoyed by these more rapidly developing societies. After this exposure, the participant may be able to bring back to his own country a set of goals and, hopefully, an understanding of the techniques and methods by which development can be achieved.

National or domestic programs also have desirable features. They make possible a curriculum more directly suited to the needs of the local trade union and the development of a local program specifically tailored to meet those needs. They avoid the distractions of luxurious living that all too frequently accompany exposure to more highly developed societies and the danger of embracing the high living standard of labor leaders in advanced countries rather than the *techniques* by which that standard was achieved. (This particular evil can be avoided, of course, by locating international centers in developing countries. But even then, there tend to be problems that are avoided by national courses—among others, the disparities of language and the inability to communicate fully in one common tongue.) National programs also do not have the problem of holding back the students from countries with advanced trade-union movements in order fully to inform the participants from countries where trade unions are a new phenomenon. They also avoid the need for costly travel subsidies, and thereby permit the finances to be concentrated on the substantive aspects of training.

These arguments do not justify either national or international programs to the exclusion of the other, and they are advanced with full realization that both types will undoubtedly continue to exist. Nonetheless, certain desirable features of each approach might be borne in mind when planning future programs. For instance, national programs, with their unique and valuable curriculum tailored to the specific needs of trade unions in the given country at a level appropriate to the trade unionists, would be valuable preparation for subsequent expansion to a full-scale mass education program.

International courses might serve more effectively if they were used for advanced study after completion of available domestic courses. With this goal in mind, the Labor Education Center of the University of the Philippines requires that applicants for its national resident program complete introductory courses offered locally. Similarly, completion of studies at the Philippine program is a prerequisite for attendance at the Center's Asian program. By establishing such criteria for admission to the international course, the sponsor assures that the participant is more mature, properly trained, and hopefully, highly motivated to perform his best in the international programs. These multinational programs would thus be able to raise their standards of admission, make more effective comparative studies of labor movements in the participating countries, and expose the participants to advanced societies with less fear that the "wrong" lessons will be absorbed. Such was the reasoning of the ORIT Institute when it urged that participants in its Mexico City Labor Educator course be "graduates" of its national seminars. The same objective is sought by the Kampala and Calcutta courses, when they encourage their graduates to establish local labor education programs. In fact, all international programs urge their participants to share the lessons they have learned in this way. In the case of Kampala, for instance, there is a concerted effort by the college's staff to initiate local training programs run by staff members and graduates. These local courses are hoped to be the basic training and prerequisite for international study.

The multiplicity of international programs has led some to contend that it would be more efficient, as well as financially desirable, to permit only one international labor training center for each continent or subcontinental region. However appealing this argument may be, it overlooks the fact that different sponsors of labor training have different goals and would not necessarily be willing to forego their stake in the field. The need for labor training is enormous and can hardly be met by one or even a dozen centers in a particular area. A choice of locations for an individual seeking training should remain, if we are to continue true to our ideal of freedom of choice in a pluralistic society. With both national and international programs in trade-union leadership training, there would be much wider geographical distribution of labor education, and more training in depth for labor officials under the national programs would be possible.

Centralized vs. Regional Teaching

Similar arguments could be made on the issue of whether training should be centralized or carried on at many locations in the field. Although this does not appear to be an issue in all the centers, it is a problem often faced by worker-education programs in the developing nations of the world. Favoring centralized programs are the arguments that they make possible ease of administration, reduced costs, and the sharing of diverse experience and backgrounds, even within a national program. In addition, there is the argument that such a center would have a favorable impact on the community in which it was located. The presence of the ICFTU Asian Labor College in Calcutta has undoubtedly been a prime factor in the establishment of several independent local worker-education centers by its alumni. Similarly, the establishment of the African Labor College in Kampala seems to have had an affirmative effect on the attitude of local British labor officers toward trade unions and their leaders. While central training centers are desirable, it should be noted that field training is also extremely valuable. It should be remembered above all that local or rural training is more likely to reach the trade-union rank and file who are most desperately in need of enlightenment concerning their rights and responsibilities. And local training can also help to meet the need for general education, by offering simple literacy training.

Local training programs can be conducted in the local vernacular and in the context of a specific industry or of specific local problems. They also permit education while at work, without the problem of financing the student's family while he is gone to a centralized training school. And local programs can provide most effective teaching in the techniques of democracy. But the cost figure might be increased because of the need to finance multiple facilities, extra travel expenses for the staff, and the like.

Certainly, there is merit to both views. One idea that might be feasible for local training is that of a joint work-study arrangement, encompassing a period of formal study, a work period during which the lessons could be put to practical use, and then a second study period to review the student's experiences and problems in his work and to equip him with further education for his next foray into the world of labor relations. This approach, used by more than fifty colleges in the United States, could have far-reaching and desirable results when applied to trade-union training.

Length of the Course

The length of time available to a union member to participate in training is also important in planning training programs. From the educator's point of view, a course for a year or more would be most desirable, since it permits full adaptability to the new school environment, covering as many subjects as possible in depth, and "amortization" of the investment in travel funds and selection time. Unfortunately, however, the difficulties of running the unions during the students' attendance at the course and the desire to expose as many union members as is practical to the center's courses have resulted in most centers offering a three- or four-month course, which is considered sufficiently long to permit coverage of the more pressing problems, but not so long that the participants will return home to find their union jobs in jeopardy. It also avoids making them into "professional students" who stray further and further from their day-to-day union responsibilities, losing their feel for the members' problems.

Total utilization of resident facilities throughout the calendar year is also of prime importance. Most centers are now able to handle at least two courses a year, using the facilities for seminars and short courses when they are available. Again, the combined work-study program is a valuable way to meet the pressing demands on the union leaders' time while building up their skills. It permits them to keep in contact with their members and to fulfill their responsibilities, and at the same time to put into practice the lessons they are learning.

Size of the Student Body

Another important structural problem, one facing all educational institutions, is that of the size of the student body. In the case of short field courses, the maximum enrollment is virtually unlimited, held in bounds only by the physical capacity of the meeting place or by the lung capacity of teachers. The longer courses are limited in size by the resident facilities of the center. At present, the average course enrollment is forty, at the international centers. Excessively large classes destroy personal contact between teacher and student, as well as among the students themselves. They also prevent group discussion techniques and the personal involvement so essential to effective teaching. Very small classes are costly in terms of overhead and staff and do not adequately meet the enormous need. Most centers have arrived at the figure of forty as most desirable for total enrollment in resident training courses. The Afro-Asian Institute in Israel, which has had an enrollment of sixty-three students, divides them into two language groups so that each group has less than forty participants. The smaller enrollment may be more effective in terms of educational impact, but perhaps this is a luxury that trade-union training centers cannot yet afford.

Staffing the Centers

The effectiveness of the training centers naturally is closely related to the quality of the instructors. At present, teaching staffs for the centers are selected primarily from the academic life or from the trade-union movement. Those from the former have the desirable qualities of objective analytical ability, diversified background, articulateness, and experience in education and teaching. On the other hand, they seldom possess the intimate knowledge of the trade-union problems confronting their students, and because of differing social and educational backgrounds, they are often aloof from their students. Trade unionists, by contrast, have a practical background in union problems, power struggles, and internal operations and can readily develop a rapport with their students. But they frequently lack teaching experience and the knowledge of theoretical aspects of labor problems that is necessary for effective planning and operations.

Many labor training centers have endeavored to find faculty members with experience in both fields, or at least trained individuals who have had some experience with the trade-union movement. Thus, government officials and attorneys, for instance, have taken part in training activities. The ideal instructor would be the trade unionist with academic training, but such specialists are difficult to find. The New York State School of Industrial and Labor Relations at Cornell University has started an International Labor Training Program specifically to provide competent trade unionists with the academic preparation necessary to enable them to serve as instructors in labor training programs or as full-time trade-union officials in the international field. Early indications are that this program, begun in 1960, will make valuable contributions to the all-important labor training field. Several graduates of the first two courses are already teaching at various international centers.

Lacking a sufficient number of such well-suited instructors, most training centers have preferred trade unionists rather than pure academicians as teachers. In most cases, these trade unionists have had little, if any, teaching experience and sometimes little formal education. Nonetheless, they have proved to be effective because of their intimate knowledge of the practical and dynamic nature of the subject. The nature of the material taught makes it easier to approach it as a general unit rather than through the fragmented subject-by-subject method that often characterizes the academic approach. Increasingly, efforts are made to encourage trade unionists to assume this new teaching function. Many centers now provide courses on techniques of labor education so that graduates can spread their lessons among a wider audience. Already several centers are fortunate enough to have teachers or tutors who are themselves graduates of the centers and have thus been exposed to both the practical and academic aspects of leadership training.

In those few centers that rely on academic instructors with no trade-union background, efforts are made to expose them, if only for a short time, to functioning trade unions, but such temporary exposure is hardly a substitute for active participation in trade-union life. It is fair to conclude that teachers with a solid trade-union background are preferable to the academicians. If active trade unionists participate in training programs of the type considered here, we shall be assured of increasingly proficient training staffs.

Financing

In Chapter 5, we discussed the problem of limited resources available to trade unions for financing worker-education programs. Without repeating the dangers of removing the programs from union control, it is necessary to consider at this point how, as a practical matter, trade-union training centers are or should be financed.

Clearly, the centers cannot be self-supporting by the participants paying sums sufficient to cover the operating costs of the program—indeed, it is not feasible to expect them to pay anything at all. Since most who attend have families, the greatest problem is to assure that funds will be available to support the families. If the participant is fortunate enough to get paid leave during his attendance, the funds are usually diverted to the family. If no such funds are provided, it is incumbent upon the sponsor of the course to provide financial aid to the participant's family.

There is a great deal of merit to the view that sacrifice for one's education gives it that much more meaning. Some of the trade-union centers, particularly in their domestic programs, expect the participants to cover their personal expenses or at least provide for their own transportation. This certainly is a desirable requirement of self-help, but it can cause great financial difficulty. When, as in India, the government offers what appears to be a similar program with no such requirement, there might well be a damaging effect on attendance at the trade-union course. Nevertheless, even if participants are required to make some personal contribution to the cost of their education, it is obvious that the contribution is insignificant in terms of the total cost of running the center. Indeed, the centers have come to realize that they must not only pay their own operating expenses but, in almost all cases, also compensate the participants. To cover these enormous costs, the centers must themselves find support from other sources.

Such support could be either material or financial. Some trade-union training centers have developed arrangements with local educational institutions to ease their financial burdens, using university or school classrooms and dormitories, teaching staffs, and a cooperative arrangement for handling administrative costs. Similar support could be offered by voluntary, commercial, or international nongovernmental organizations, if they felt the work of the centers to be of mutual benefit. As for direct financial assistance, arrangements might be made to obtain financial grants "with no strings attached" or money for scholarships from foundations, political parties, or local, regional, or national governments. In addition, introduction of legislation requiring employers to provide for paid leaves of absence to those attending educational courses of this type would relieve trade unions and their members of the responsibility of supporting the participants and their families. Such leaves would be, in effect, a community scholarship paid for by the employers. Some countries have passed such legislation and have qualified labor education courses as justifying payment of the leave.

In accepting direct government financing, either in scholarships or in grants to the center, certain caveats are entered: First, government money too loosely spent in this field merely antagonizes the recipient and his associates and gives them the impression that such extravagant offerings are more like bribes than altruistic donations. Second, the recipients of such largess may well be viewed by their fellow trade unionists as having "sold out" to the providing government. Third, government financing will usually be limited to those individuals who have been approved by the local government and will often bypass the most worthy candidates because they may belong to a politically unacceptable union or an opposition political group. Lastly, government support of graduates of training centers while they are teaching raises some problems in conflict of loyalty—to the provider of the subsidy and to the trade-union movement of which the graduate is a member. A course entirely supported by the government is likely to attract trade unionists who might otherwise attend a union-financed course. Such problems are certainly very real, but they should not detract from the awareness of the need for more effective cooperation to meet mutually desirable objectives.

Although this examination of structural problems may provide some directives for judging what type of program may be most effective, it presents only one problem faced by sponsors of training centers. Let us now turn to another—the equally difficult one of selecting the participants for leadership training.

7. SELECTING THE PARTICIPANTS

The success of labor training projects depends on selecting participants who are capable of absorbing the material taught, who are likely to be active contributors to class discussions, and who will put into practice the lessons learned when they return to their unions. The selection process has three important elements that merit detailed examination: Who does the selecting? What criteria are used? And, what type of student group is the result? Let us consider these elements in turn.

The Selectors

In selecting participants, as elsewhere, "he who pays the fiddler calls the tune." More precisely, the sponsor of the training center has ultimate control over the selection procedure: The selection will be made by the trade unions where they run the program, or by the governments where they do. But there are still a wide variety of selection procedures. In the past, the power of selection rested ultimately with the sponsors, although it was often delegated to union and government officials at the home of the participant, and perhaps more effectively, to the administrators and the staffs of the centers themselves. But, regardless of whether the sponsorship is public or private, there tends to be ineffective selection when it is delegated to local officials. Although they are no doubt fully apprised of the criteria for admission to the centers, they frequently minimize the importance of such criteria and introduce their own, more personalized versions—probably the greatest danger to the maintenance of effective standards at the centers. While concentrating selection powers at the center itself reduces some of the problems, it does not overcome all the problems that arise.

The local leaders of trade unions are generally devoted and conscientious. As noted earlier, they sometimes tend to consider the several months spent at the courses as just that much time away from the pressing needs of the union, rather than as an investment in more competent leadership, while others tend to send the members who "never will be missed" and who are unlikely to profit from the course. Even some of the most conscientious officials are likely to fear that the courses will stimulate potential rivals for union leadership. There are, of course, union (and government) officials who consider the trade unions simply as organizations useful to their own careers and who do not always possess the right perspective on labor training. They cause considerable harm by sending either those to whom they owe political favors or those whose favor they would like to curry. They seldom view labor training as an opportunity to stimulate a dynamic trade-union movement within their country.

If local government personnel do the choosing, they are confronted not only with these same problems, but also others created by the tendency of trade-union officials to be active in politics. An ambitious trade-union leader, if given further training, might constitute a vital political force as well as an economic one. With the prospect of stimulating future political rivals, even professionals in the ministries of labor would be quite careful to ascertain whether a candidate's political behavior would accrue to the benefit of the incumbent political party or the opposition.

It would seem logical that the administrator of each center should have control over who is to study there. In both trade-union and government centers, the administrative staff is sufficiently aware of the desired caliber of students and has sufficient faith in the objectives of the sponsor to decide what kind of student should be enrolled. Unfortunately, however, the administrators do not know which candidates in the large geographical area they serve can meet the criteria. Unless they have spent considerable time at work in the field, they are likely to be unacquainted with the best prospects. Generally, they do not do the selecting themselves but, at best, select on the basis of written applications and recommendations from local personnel, thus sharing their selection power.

Selection by staff members in an exclusively domestic program is quite feasible, because of the staff's constant contact with the unions and their knowledge of who would profit most from the course. But if the staff were to select the participants in an international program, they would undoubtedly do so on the basis of written applications, coupled, perhaps, with recommendations from local government or union officials. Such written evidence is far from sufficient to determine whether a student will contribute to, as well as profit from, a training program. The best selector is the person who knows both the potential participant and the demands of the program. Here, the personal interview is, of course, of great value. But in the existing centers, only a limited number of interviews has been possible. Many staff members from the Kampala, Mexico City, Washington, and Calcutta centers have, though, traveled in their regions, alert to possible contact with prospective pupils. In the Philippines, field representatives conducting local training programs meet and investigate nominees from the short-term courses and make recommendations to the staff at Manila. But this technique has not been used consistently, and there is no evidence that the staffs of any of the centers have been able to interview all their applicants, or even all the accepted students before their matriculation. Even if this were physically possible, it is questionable whether staff members have the political knowledge and sagacity necessary to deal with competing national centers and competing countries and governments without antagonizing the very institutions they are in the long run endeavoring to assist.

For these reasons, it seems more realistic to place the responsibility for selection with the sponsors rather than the staff or administrators of the centers. Although their knowledge of the workings of the center itself—its techniques of teaching, its standards of excellence, and so on—may be limited, they have the advantage of being able to reach the potential students easily, and of being sure that in selecting the participants they are working directly toward producing the type of union leader they think is most desirable. The staff members are, or should be, continually engaged in teaching and research. In most cases, they are geographically confined to their center and its environs, and lack experience in the areas from which their students come. It would be well-nigh impossible, for example, for the staff of the Israeli Institute to travel everywhere in Asia and Africa to meet and evaluate prospective students. It is far more economical and convenient to have Israeli government officials in each country seek out interested trade unionists and then inform the staff of the Institute in Tel Aviv of their availability and desirability.

Similarly, in the case of programs carried out by the United States Government, it is expedient to have the participants selected by the resident U.S. Operations Mission. The Missions are informed of the programs by the administering agency in Washington; they are aware of both the requirements of the program and the availability of students, also of the internal problems in any given country and its union movements. They are familiar with the available candidates and aware of the impact that the training should or can have on them, their trade union, and their country.

With private programs, there seems to be the same justification for selection by the sponsoring organization. Although trade unions cannot maintain the world-wide administrative network that governments do, regional organizations—such as those of the ICFTU, for instance—are generally aware of the needs for training and of available talent for such training in the affiliated national unions. Through their international or regional offices, the trade unions can maintain a certain degree of uniformity in their selection standards despite the fact that they, like the U.S. mission staffs, are actually once removed from the actual workings of the training centers themselves.

They, too, lack the intimate knowledge of the immediate needs of the centers, and are prone to think more in terms of the problems and benefits for the local situation.

Mention must also be made of those instances where selection is kept exclusively under the control of the host country, either through its national union centers or by the government. In the case of trade-union programs, the training centers and the administering union regional organizations are often powerless to accept any one but the participants designated by the local national union. When selection is left exclusively in the hands of the national unions, there is a strong likelihood that they will apply criteria that are incompatible with the needs of the training centers. Internal union politics are controlling and there may be frequent disregard for the objectives of the training centers. Such was the problem at both the Calcutta and Kampala colleges, in the period before they or their regional organizations exercised any control over the selection process.

A similar result obtains in government programs where there are no local selection affiliates. For instance, in the Philippine Asian program, the U.S. Government was frequently unable to control the selection criteria when there was no local USOM, and the selection process was carried out by national governments or ministries of labor. In such cases, the weaknesses of local trade-union selection were magnified by the political or economic considerations of the government concerned. The ILO Institute, with its system of organizational or governmental endorsement, has some of the same problems, although applicants are free to apply to the Institute directly.

Fortunately, however, an increase in the number of applicants and a greater awareness of the requirements for successful training courses have reduced the likelihood of an inadequate student body. As the centers developed and their reputations expanded, they soon achieved a greater degree of control over the composition of the student body. Local selection agencies of the trade unions or governments sought more places for their members; the increased number of nominees resulted in a transfer of the locus for final selection to the training centers themselves. Since the centers maintained a kind of veto power over the nominees, the increasing tide of applications soon afforded them a real power of selection. In some cases, they were able to choose one out of four applications. The continued growth in their reputation makes it likely that they will continue to exercise this power.

In addition to this transfer of control over selection, the development of the centers into viable institutions has, to a certain extent, freed the staff members from perpetual duty in the classroom. At the Kampala College, the American Institute, and the Philippine programs, for instance, the establishment of extension departments makes it feasible for some of the staff to devote more time to travel through their region, for the purpose of interviewing prospective candidates and informing local nominating bodies of the criteria to be used in selection. Although the knowledge of applicants obtained in this manner tends to be superficial, the travel at least permits greater exposure to and evaluation of the potential candidates than is possible in correspondence. The Afro-Asian Institute, which did send one staff member on a recruiting trip before its first course, now endeavors to send staff members to participating countries to raise the standard of selection there as well as to become acquainted with the substantive labor problems in each. Staff members from the American Institute traveling in Latin America to check on the progress of graduates frequently come in contact with potential students as well. It is fair to conclude that those responsible for choosing potential participants for the training centers—union or government officials of the country from which the students come, or international labor or other government officials—are gradually changing from selectors to nominators. They are transferring much of their power of final selection to the administrators of the schools themselves. One cannot assume that the transfer is complete, or, if it is, that the selection is perfect, for there still remains the important question of the criteria that both nominators and selectors, trade unions and governments, apply.

Criteria for Selection

In considering the question of what standards should be used, we often find that a double set of standards is employed. The first could be described as the ideal standards, and are found in the published documents of the training centers. The second might be described as the practical, realistic standards necessary to use in getting participants here and now. Obviously, the latter are less stringent than the former. The printed criteria are usually quite explicit: language ability, a certain amount of formal education, experience in the trade-union movement, as well as the more abstract requirements of non-Communist leadership, integrity, devotion to trade unionism, intelligence, and so on. Each of these requirements is quite reasonable and well-suited to the needs of the centers.

Proficiency in the language used in the training courses is obviously essential. Most of the participants come from communities where English, French, or even Spanish is, at best, a second or only official language. It is true that, wherever possible, the courses should be taught in the local language, especially when one realizes that some of the trade unionists with the greatest potential for leadership may never have had the opportunity for formal training in a European language, and that either opportunists or members of the intellectual elite using the unions as a personal vehicle are the only possible candidates for training in a center that requires knowledge of a European language. Nevertheless, the fact remains that English, French, and Spanish *are* the official languages in most of the less developed countries; they are taught in the schools; they are used in commerce, communications, and collective bargaining. They are also international languages, and in using them, students from several countries can be taught at one time. Accordingly, it becomes necessary to conduct training courses in whichever of these is suited to the region or country concerned. In some cases, the centers have programs that are offered bilingually. In the case of the ILO Institute, a bilingual arrangement in English and French has been developed, but suffers from the fact that some of the students come from Latin American countries and are fluent in neither French nor English—a limitation that greatly reduces the Latin American student body.

Proficiency in the language of the training centers is therefore the key to effective participation in the programs. Instruction in the language of any given center is the only way by which trade unionists from a variety of cultures, backgrounds, and countries can share their experiences with other trade unionists.

A certain amount of formal education is equally important. It is not merely a question of gaining literacy, for formal academic education is also of great value in giving the trade unionist an understanding of his environment and his own potential and in teaching him many of the skills he will need as a union official. Some centers require a secondary school education, but in most instances a lower educational level is acceptable, for it is unrealistic to expect many trade unionists from emerging countries to have had more than a rudimentary formal education.

As for the trade-union experience demanded of participants, the standards can be more objectively applied. Most international courses seek students who have demonstrated, by their experience and activities before applying for admission, their potential as union leaders. Only through such evidence is it possible to assess the impact the applicant is likely to have on his union after he has completed training.

Another common requirement of these courses is demonstrated loyalty to free trade unionism and antitotalitarianism. It is the purpose of this requirement, found at most centers, to prevent infiltration of those opposed to the ideal of democratic trade unionism or dedicated to its destruction. Attendance in these programs often comes as a reward for ideological loyalty, especially when the sponsors restrict selection to members of affiliated or anti-Communist unions. As a result, non-Communists in trade unions led by Communists or considered pro-Communist are denied the opportunity for training. We deny them and the "fence-sitting Communists" just that training that might arm them sufficiently to maintain their independence from Communist control, that, in fact, might encourage them to take affirmative measures to remove the Communist leadership from their unions.

In considering the other, more abstract criteria established by the training centers, it is difficult to establish an objective standard for judgment. The evidence that a candidate meets the criteria must come from the subjective comments of the applicant himself, his superiors in his union or employment, or his sponsors or recommenders.

Even when established criteria for selection do exist, the training centers often have had to overlook them in accepting many of their students. Often these waivers have been nominal: overlooking formal education for a particularly experienced trade unionist; or hoping that dubious proficiency in English could be strengthened by attendance at the training center. Such variation in the selection criteria is natural. A far greater problem arises when many or all of the published standards are adapted (or, more realistically, lowered) to meet the abilities of the applicants. Unfortunately, this is often true.

In the matter of language proficiency, administrators of many centers have indicated that their students have not met the expected standards. This is probably due to an unintentional overestimation of language ability by the applicant himself or by his sponsors. Reasoning that his English, French, or Spanish was good enough for general communication and business dealings, he assumes it will be sufficiently strong for studies. Unfortunately, however, many students find that their superficial familiarity with the language is inadequate when more detailed study in it is required. While they may be able to converse or answer questions, they are often reluctant to initiate comments and, because of their self-consciousness, tend to remain aloof from group discussions. The disparity between the articulate and the silent, and the bright and the backward is accentuated in the classrooms.

One way of overcoming this problem is to conduct the classes at the level of the students with the lowest language proficiency. This, of course, destroys interest in the course and lowers its value to the students with high language proficiency. Another means of solving the problem is to offer the students an intensive language course before the training programs begin, so that they can strengthen their language abilities sufficiently to become effective participants in the courses. This device falls short of fully meeting the needs, because it is often hard to determine in advance which participants need and should be invited to have this training, and because, in many cases, the students are unaware of or unwilling to admit their language deficiencies.

The Philippine Center has introduced simultaneous translation to meet the needs of the students from non-English speaking countries. While this is expensive and cumbersome (particularly when translation into many languages is required), it is probably the most effective device for bringing trade-union leadership training to those who, regardless of linguistic skill, are likely to profit most from it.

Mention should be made of the unique contribution made by Israel in this connection. Although Hebrew is the national language of the Histadrut program, it is not spoken anywhere in Africa or elsewhere in Asia, and it is difficult to teach enough of the language to have Africans and Asians take effective part in class discussions. Teaching Hebrew might still have provided a somewhat cumbersome answer, but the Israelis sought to adapt the program to the languages spoken by most of the students. They started a simultaneous program in English and French, in which lecturers from the University of Tel Aviv and Hebrew University delivered the same lectures in both languages. In addition, French-speaking and English-speaking tutors worked personally with students during the course, so that their knowledge of these languages grew sufficiently for them successfully to absorb the material offered. The only language bar was in communication between the students of different language groups, and Hebrew, jokingly referred to as the language of Pan-Africanism, frequently served as the link.

Similar problems are faced in regard to the requirements of trade-union experience and formal education. If there were strict adherence to these criteria, the classes at the centers would be small indeed, for attendance at secondary schools in Asia, Africa, and Latin America is comparatively rare. Those who complete secondary school are often swept into white-collar jobs; comparatively few trade-union oriented people achieve this level of education and the few that do are unlikely to resist the pleasant attractions of a company or government labor-relations post to remain within the labor movement. Even those without formal education but with wide practical experience in the trade-union movement are in great demand in management and government. Accordingly, there are but a few union officials with both formal education and practical trade-union experience, and those who possess both requirements are often in top positions in their unions and unavailable for courses at training centers. It is therefore necessary for the sponsors of the training centers to gloss over the formal requirements for admission in order to select a number of students with lesser qualifications to fill the needs of the courses. The reduction in standards becomes substantive rather than procedural. As a result, the level of instruction is obviously lowered, so that those with insufficient practical or academic background can keep abreast of the material offered. This has happened to at least some extent in all the centers, but the lowering of standards is not due solely to the failure of the staff to select only those who meet the formal requirements. It is due even more to the pragmatic approach used by sponsors in nominating and selecting participants.

Ignoring the need to meet specific criteria for admission to labor training centers is the most damaging element in the whole selection process, particularly when the selection is made by local trade-union or government officials. It can happen in a trade-union course where each affiliated union is entitled to send one or more students, or where the quota is determined according to industry rather than geographical region, in which case a less qualified student may be selected to fulfill a quota while two highly qualified candidates from another region are rejected.

The same quota problems arise in government programs. Here, they are further complicated by political considerations. For example, the U.S. Government may provide a training opportunity for a union leader of a particular country only to find that his government must offer a similar opportunity to representatives of other unions if it is to maintain its impartiality. This appears to have occurred under the Indian Government program, where the four national unions are included, despite the obvious reluctance of some government officials to have the Communist union involved. Another problem is the likelihood that the government official will select the trade unionists who, it is felt, will not cause "trouble" on their return.

The Selected Group

By and large, the courses have done quite well in attracting the type of student that their official criteria indicate they seek. The increased interest in the courses has resulted in more and more competent trade unionists applying to them, thus enabling the staff of the centers and those entrusted with final selection to "weed out" the unwanted candidates. Political officials have changed their attitude and are coming to realize the importance of an effective trade-union movement as a partner in achieving the political goals of the new countries. Similarly, the trade-union leaders have changed their attitude—partly because the early graduates of the centers more and more often achieved positions of leadership in their unions. Thus, they can strengthen their unions' full support of the training programs and see to it that competent individuals are directed toward participation.

Much improvement is still needed in the basic problem of language proficiency, and, in the international courses, of achieving a balance in the level of competence of the participants. More attention must be devoted to assuring that the students from countries with advanced trade-union structures are not held back by those from countries with new and essentially primitive trade-union structures, or that the former do not control the courses at the expense of the latter.

If improvement of the selection processes continues, it is possible that the substantive problems of the courses can be readily overcome. Changes in the selection process have been made rapidly, and for the better. They augur well for the future of the existing training centers and serve as bench marks for establishing selection criteria for new ones.

8. CURRICULUM

The subject matter taught in the training centers concerns the information and techniques for the future development of trade unions. This is the substantive material for the teaching of which the centers have been created. The subject matter, in contrast to the democracy that is the ultimate goal of the teaching, is imposed from above; there is little opportunity for the participants to indicate a course of study they might want. Indeed, surveys to discover the needs of a particular group of students, so that a curriculum may be adapted to meet those needs, are infrequent. This lack of grass-roots initiative is generally the fault of the courses' sponsors, and is attributable to their valid belief that they know what the problems and needs are in developing trade unions.

There are obviously variations in the approach used in the centers when determining the curriculum. The fundamental differences between government-sponsored and trade-union training programs come once again to the forefront—should the courses stress the role of trade unions in economic development or the need to build autonomous trade unions through dues collection, collective bargaining, and the like?

Proponents of the view that unions should be committed participants in economic development stress that curricula must be oriented toward explaining the trade unionists' stake in national society and the need for personal sacrifice while the economy undergoes development. Courses in economic development theory, labor legislation, conciliation, productivity, and cooperation should reign supreme, emphasizing the team spirit that is so essential to universal support for, and unanimity of purpose in, economic development. Although government-sponsored programs are the most likely to adopt this approach, it is also evident that such a curriculum would be emphasized in programs jointly sponsored by labor, management, and government.

Criticism of this approach is not intended to imply disdain for government participation in labor education or to minimize the need for labor-management harmony in economic development, but rather, to highlight the contrast between the government view and that of the trade unions regarding their respective programs. The curriculum of the trade-union program might include the foregoing elements, but it would emphasize practical courses needed to build union strength and so transform the unions into viable organizations.

Courses in subjects such as techniques of effective dues collection, public speaking, contract negotiation, strike techniques, and the like, while perhaps ultimately serving the goal of integrating trade unions into a national program of economic development, are essential first and foremost to the development of effective independent trade unions. Here again, the argument can be advanced that the higher standard of living for the rank and file gained through strong unions, coupled with an effective structure for personal and excise taxes, will more effectively assure growth of capital than draining off profits to accounts in Swiss banks and squandering them on conspicuous consumption.

It is difficult to prescribe the perfect curriculum for a labor training course, in view of the varying objectives of the sponsors. The first question is whether the curriculum should be "loose" or "tight." Should it be a wide-ranging study of various trade-union problems in developing countries, requiring a knowledgeable and versatile instructor? Or should it be a prearranged series of lectures concentrating on the main problems, suitable for teaching by a less knowledgeable and experienced instructor? The former permits a free choice of material to suit the needs of a diverse student body. The latter runs the risk of urging short cuts and of glossing over essentials. The ideal curriculum is probably like the one attained in the Indian Government program, where the education officers are provided with a very wide background and wealth of material which they can in turn offer to their students.

Regardless of the specific orientation of a curriculum and the specific motivation of the sponsors, certain elements must be included in all courses, although the emphasis may vary according to the objectives of the sponsor. These elements are those required to give the participant an understanding of his role in the trade union, as well as an ability to absorb other lessons and techniques.

The initial step in formulating curricula must be the preconditioning of the students. In almost all cases, the students come with a minimum of academic education and virtually no formal training in the subjects covered. They must be introduced to the most basic concepts, and the teaching should be arranged so that it starts with the concrete (i.e., the experiences they have had) and leads into the theoretical. Above all, the orientation in all courses should be to responsible leadership, for the student is being trained to be a leader.

Background material in economics is essential. This should include studies of the country's economic system and a comparative examination of other economic systems, with attention to growth plans and models. The role of wages and profits in the economy, varying methods of wage payment, and productivity should also be considered. A study of the various industries and products that contribute to a particular economy's development is also essential, to give workers from a given industry the necessary perspective on their role in society.

Similar consideration should be given to political subjects, the structure and operation of the nation's government, other forms of government, and international operations such as the UN, the ILO, and other agencies. Another worthwhile subject is the comparative study of democracy and totalitarianism, emphasizing the democratic nature of the trade-union movement—its position as a cornerstone for building a democratic nation. This is done in the sense of teaching an affirmative ideology. Several centers, particularly those sponsored by trade unions, give courses in fascist and Communist tactics, in the hope and expectation that they will prepare the students to protect their unions from takeover by the extreme right or left. Opportunity for free discussion on contemporary politics and international relations is also valuable, because it highlights the necessity for free exchange of ideas in a democratic society. Failure to provide such a "release" for politically active minds can cause irreparable harm to the entire program of a center proclaiming support of democratic ideals.

The study of labor organizations is equally important. This should include a study of the structure of the country's national trade unions, of regional trade-union groups, the ICFTU, IFCTU, ITS, and the World Federation of Trade Unions (WFTU). In courses where students come from several different countries, a comparative study of their several labor organizations would prove beneficial to all.

The study of labor-management relations is essential for all courses. This should include examination of the labor-management balance of power, the role and use of collective bargaining, techniques of negotiation, the grievance procedure and its use, industrial discipline, and other matters of contract administration and enforcement. Government-sponsored labor training centers in countries with large government sectors might be reluctant to embark on the study of some of these, but they are essential, if the trade unionist is to be able to build up his union, or if the union is to deal effectively with private management. Even a nation with a large government sector would be expected to strive toward some negotiating relationship with its employees, if only to ascertain the trouble spots in the operations, particularly in the parts of the government sector that are often considered to be beyond the usual state administrative powers, such as steel mills, railroads, and the like.

Examination of labor legislation is another necessary course in worker education, particularly in underdeveloped areas where, as in Latin America, a whole code of protective laws protects the worker, but where, because of lack of training, he is usually ignorant of the rights he is guaranteed—by minimum-wage and maximum-hour legislation, social security, workmen's compensation, safety, old-age insurance, and social welfare laws. Also important are laws providing for conciliation and other methods of dispute settlement, which must be pointed out to the rank and file if they are to be cognizant of their full rights. This is imperative, particularly in government-sponsored programs, if the programs are to fulfill their moral obligation of informing the students of the protection such laws provide.

Certain other items can be grouped under the general heading of union administration, and are also worthy of study. When offered in a government program, however, consideration of these matters may ultimately strengthen the independence of the unions to a point the sponsors consider impolitic. Instruction in bookkeeping, parliamentary procedure, use of the library, gathering labor statistics, performing research, public speaking, and running union meetings are all essential to the development of unions as democratic institutions participating in the building of a country.

Labor education techniques is another essential subject, for the same reasons, and also for assuring the maximum impact of labor training on the local rank and file.

Some sponsors will obviously be reluctant to include subjects such as effective dues collection, and strike techniques, but these are also an important part of labor training and the building of effective unions—perhaps the most important. Omission of such subjects from a curriculum does not merely imply that the students should get such information elsewhere, but that the subject matter has been purposely put beyond the students' reach. The students consider the proper and full role of the union to be that charted by their teachers, and, having no other sources of information, will assume that other devices and techniques are nonexistent. But those techniques are ultimately as essential to the development of responsive and responsible trade unions as are any of the more generally accepted curricular items.

In considering these possible subjects for training center curricula, it should be noted that not all of them are controversial. Most of them could be taught so as to be acceptable to management, government, and labor alike. This raises the possibility of creating new centers where specialized subjects could be taught with management, labor, and government personnel taking part. This would avoid the difficulty presently experienced by trade unions in teaching administrative skills to their members, many of whom end up in government or management.

From the question of curriculum content, let us turn to the procedural problems of teaching such a curriculum. The international centers have classes made up of trade unionists from many countries with a variety of trade-union experience at varying levels of sophistication. Accepting this variety of backgrounds as inevitable in an international course, there must be a way in which the curriculum can be adapted to it. A great deal can be learned from a comparative study of the problems awaiting the students on their return home. Thus, the study of economic and political structures and the role of the trade union in them could be approached as a comparative study of all the countries represented at the course. In this way, each student or group of students from a particular country could do independent research and study of their own economic, political, and legal systems in the context of basic principles and fundamentals initially laid down. This would do much to overcome the alleged disadvantages of bringing trade unionists with such diversified backgrounds to study at a single center. It would, however, also place heavy demands on the staff, who would be required to have specific knowledge of each country. But such a curriculum would not only free the sponsors from the charge that they seek to pattern regional trade-union centers after that of their own country, but would also alleviate the doubts of those who reluctantly support international programs because of the lack of sufficient finances to sustain national programs. Indeed, there would appear to be greater educational advantage in a course of comparative studies than in a regimented recital of the structure and problems of one particular country.

As the centers gain more experience, they begin to experiment with new ideas. One new idea that is gaining popularity is that of concentrating on specialized courses, comparable to a college "major." For instance, the Kampala College has a program which, after study of certain basic subjects, is divided in three groups: one for union organizers, one for researchers, and one for labor educators. Other specialized courses are offered at various centers for labor journalists, cooperative administrators, financial secretaries, and so on.

Most centers have placed special emphasis on training teachers of labor education. The orientation of the curriculum to this end is easily accomplished. Emphasizing the learning of educational techniques as a vital part of the curriculum will provide the students with the tools necessary to carry what they have learned back to the rank and file. While this technique is used successfully in the Indian Government scheme, its greatest likelihood of success appears to be in the ORIT's Mexico City program. There, the training of teachers in educational techniques and in other substantive union matters will filter back to many national centers and structures, where the ex-students will devote their major energies to establishing labor education programs. The same objective is sought by other centers as well. Since the available time is limited, the training of labor leaders in this specialized function will result in a curtailment of other aspects of their normal training, but the indications are that expansion of the curriculum in teacher-training techniques should be encouraged even if done at the expense of the substantive matters in the curriculum. When teaching techniques are imparted to the students, their own interests in the subjects will be increased, because of the responsibility involved in mastering that which must later be taught. Their interest in learning other subjects through independent study and research will be stimulated. When this process is accomplished, the success of labor training and its perpetuation are assured.

9. TEACHING TECHNIQUES

It is naturally difficult for those of us who have had twelve or sixteen or more years of education to imagine the problems of teaching advanced material to students with less educational preparation. Although the leaders of trade unions in developing countries probably have had somewhat more education than the members they represent, it is undoubtedly true that most of those who attend labor training courses do not have a strong educational background. Even we in the United States, where we enjoy a fairly comprehensive and effective educational system, are sometimes shocked to hear that many of our own citizens have never had a high school education and that our literacy rate is not the highest in the world.

Still, there is obviously a great contrast between our educational opportunities and those available in the southern half of the globe. We must awaken to this disparity in educational experience and to the obvious absence of previous preparation, or "preconditioning," that handicaps the endeavors to expand education in the developing nations. This volume is not intended as an examination of the problems of adapting teaching techniques to overcome this absence of educational preconditioning, but it is necessary to note that the problems encountered in teaching the workers are even greater than those found in the formal governmental educational systems of the new nations.

Participants in labor training programs have usually risen to positions of power in their organizations by means of extensive working experience and in spite of their lack of education. It is possible that the training programs constitute their first exposure to classroom teaching. For this reason, they tend

82

to be enthusiastic about their participation and eager to make the most of the unique opportunity that has come their way. Undoubtedly, the courses help in their general education. In addition, because the training centers are well-established institutions, frequently with impressive names, and because of the "status" that results from being a student or alumnus of such an institution, they stir the enthusiasm of others seeking admission.

It is the objective of this chapter to discuss the attempts to adapt the educational experience to the level of the student, so that, despite the pressures of time, the lack of the students' earlier exposure to classrooms, the handicaps of language, and the variations in outlook and experience among the students, it is still a meaningful experience. If it is such, it can be considered to have made a contribution to the enlightenment of the students concerned, and to have achieved the goals set by the programs' sponsors.

When most of the labor training centers were established, the natural inclination was to teach in the same way as in formal academic institutions. The founders of two centers— the Philippine and Histadrut programs—steeped in the tradition of formal academic training at advanced levels and influenced by their proximity to neighboring universities, used a teaching system based on the lecture. This was the case of virtually all the centers. Just as a program of university lectures would be unsuited to first and second graders, or even secondary school students, for that matter, so too did it prove to be unsatisfactory for the students in the labor training courses.

Although lectures are probably the most efficient means of transmitting a large amount of material, they are probably the least efficient in terms of encouraging absorption of the material covered. They require a good deal of "preconditioning." Understanding of a complex new terminology, facility in a foreign tongue, and, above all, the ability to concentrate and organize one's thoughts so as to receive and absorb a sustained argument are all prerequisites for profiting from a lecture—factors that often baffle university students, let alone unschooled trade unionists in the developing nations of the world.

It is unfortunate that lectures are the backbone of the teaching method of so many training centers, and that they have been adhered to so rigidly, despite a growing reliance in educational circles on other teaching methods. In several centers, the view has been that lectures were the most suitable technique because the greatest amount of material could be covered in them. That they were accepted by the student body was proved, it was claimed, by the fact that all students were attentive during them and that during the question period provided, their response was usually active and provocative. But on closer examination, the questions asked usually related to the subjects discussed during the final few minutes of the lecture. It is fair to conclude that the audience's rapt attention was largely due to the fact that most of the students had had no prior exposure to any of the material and perhaps even to the terminology used; that they were intent on absorbing as much as they could even if they failed to understand the introductory material or basic direction of the lecture; most of all, that they were determined to be respectful even though they did not understand or even listen to what the teacher was saying. It is true that lectures do not reach all the students, and that the teachers often assume the students' universal understanding of the material from the response of the articulate few. But this problem of assimilation could be reduced by distributing printed copies or synopses of the lectures in advance so that students could follow them more closely.

As the various centers have steered their diversified student bodies through the courses, they have come to realize the limitations on a ten-week or even four-month course and accordingly have reduced their objectives in terms of material to be covered. They have come to realize that their initial reliance solely on the lecture achieved progress at the expense of the less aggressive, less articulate students. Most centers have somewhat reluctantly concluded that more can be taught by encouraging the students to engage in cooperative discussion and research than through strict adherence to the lecture system. This realization has led to increased use of discussion groups, seminars, role playing, demonstrations and the like. The success of their introduction into labor training has been even greater than in traditional educational circles. The reduced emphasis on lectures, particularly in the international courses, has permitted greater attention to be paid to a comparative study of labor movements and problems. In several centers, discussions and seminars have stimulated the students to prepare papers on their own trade unions and to discuss them in a group program. This would be quite impractical in a formal lecture system.

Many texts have been written on modern teaching techniques in general, which should be read for their applicability to labor education. The International Labor Office has published a great deal of material on methods of workers' education in developing areas. Its compendium should be compulsory reading for those interested in this field. It deals with the pros and cons of lectures, discussion groups, panels, debates, group work, written material, montages, maps, blackboards, charts, radio, recordings, television, films, filmstrips, field trips, etc. Since its catalog is so detailed and comprehensive, there is no need to reiterate the views and approaches it describes. Suffice it to say that the introduction of such techniques into the training of trade-union leadership brings rapid and rewarding results.

There are several comments on improvised teaching techniques that do deserve particular attention.

There is one teaching technique used in a labor training center that has not been used in the formal educational institutions of the industrialized world. Rather, it developed as a result of the lack of success of the lecture system. This is the modified seminar approach adopted by V. S. Mathur and used in the ICFTU's Asian Labor College.* Material to be cov-

* See Mathur's "Workers' Education in Asia," *International Labor Review*, LXXXIII, No. 6 (June, 1961), 554–75.

ered is divided into short topics, each of which is discussed in small groups of students who, under a tutor's direction, prepare a working paper on the subject based on the discussions and on reading of suggested material. The working papers are read aloud by each group to a meeting of the entire student body, and a formal summary of the material developed. The staff emphasizes important items and inserts those that have been slighted or omitted. When this is completed, the students have a more thorough knowledge of the material because they have taken an active part in writing the working papers and have personally been responsible for transmitting their content from the printed page to the working paper. They are then in a more knowledgeable position to listen to a formal "wrap-up" lecture on the entire subject they have studied. In many cases, they are even prepared for guest lectures by specialists who might otherwise have communicated with only a small portion of the audience.

The most effective methods for teaching students of a practical bent who may not have had sufficient exposure to traditional education are undoubtedly demonstrations and role-playing. Each is valuable because it permits the students to take an active part in the educational process and gives them that essential measure of practical experience that can be instantly recalled when they confront similar situations in their own work at home.

Although all the centers mentioned here do use the role-playing technique (which may be considered as a form of demonstration) in teaching negotiation techniques, how to run a union meeting, process a grievance, or present an arbitration case, few emphasize them in the many cases where they are most usable. This is regrettable, for demonstrations permit a particular subject to be approached from all relevant angles. This multiplicity of approaches is often lacking in a stiff item-by-item classroom analysis. The ICFTU centers run mock picket lines complete with placards and occasional "run-ins" with the "management"; the Afro-Asian Institute devotes several weeks to field work, during which students actually work in companies, cooperatives, or trade-union offices of their own industry. The most impressive use of demonstrations takes place in the dock-workers' residential area of Calcutta, where the ICFTU's Asian Labor College established a Workers' Education Center.* The Center is an ideal teaching aid for the college's students, pointing up the value of local labor education, the ease in establishing and running them, and the interest of the rank and file in taking part in their activities. It also serves as a laboratory for testing new teaching techniques, and enables the students at the college to spend a few hours in practice teaching. If each student in the Asian Labor College endeavored to duplicate the Center when he returned home, the trade-union movement could be credited with making a substantial contribution to teaching some of the principles of democratic procedure, reducing illiteracy among the adult rank and file, and improving the cultural lives of the otherwise forgotten workers of a dozen Asian countries.

One largely unexplored area in labor training is education in the use of mass media. Although this subject is not a part of any of the centers' curriculums, it would be quite practical and valuable to teach the students how to publicize their unions and attract new members through press, publications, radio, tapes, slides, films, and so on. Some centers have encouraged their graduates to carry on the work of the Center when they return home, and have supplied them with printed study guides and material for distribution. The centers have generally refrained from formally teaching techniques in this field but they have included them in demonstration devices. For instance, in preparing and issuing a student newspaper, the students can learn the lessons of newspaper administration and how to operate a mimeograph machine—knowledge that could later be put to good use. Similarly, an exercise in translating available English, French, or Spanish publications into their own language would create a wealth of useful material for distribution to the local rank and file. It would also

* See Appendix B.

instruct the translators and stimulate them into distributing their translations on returning home. Of course, the printed material is not necessarily the most effective but is certainly the least expensive and probably most durable of the available materials that can be used in this type of work. In Uganda, the trade unions have succeeded in periodically obtaining radio time to expound their views—an easy method for leaders who are used to addressing audiences, even if not unseen ones. The value of this radio work lies more in its impact on management and the general public than its effect on the rank and file, who may lack radio receivers or not be sophisticated enough to understand the nature of the broadcast, and who will be captivated by the personality or voice of the speaker rather than by his message. Some thought should be given to organizing worker education courses on radio—or television, where available. With a well prepared syllabus and proctors at the classrooms where the receivers are located, it would be possible to bring training courses in a few hours to more students than one center could handle in a decade.

The most desirable teaching techniques now used at the labor training centers are undoubtedly the audio-visual ones. The cheapest technique is the use of the flannel board, the blackboard, or colored crayons or "magic markers" and paper. At a more expensive level are films; at Kampala and certain other centers, the students are taught how to operate motion-picture projectors. But there are comparatively few available films that would have meaning to trade unionists of Africa, Asia, or Latin America. The local information agencies of the U.K., West Germany, Israel, France, and the U.S.A. do have films on union activities in those countries, but comparatively little footage is obtainable on local union problems, and, in any case, there is frequently a shortage of film projectors. In addition, most material is not available in the local language. A complete audio-visual laboratory, however, set up at the Philippine center, has produced tapes, filmstrips, slides, and motion pictures for its extension programs. The staff has also instructed their students in the preparation and use of such materials on their own. Although the cost of developing such an audio-visual center may be great, there is no doubt that funds should be made available for this purpose elsewhere. They produce materials in the workers' own language dealing with specific local problems of great significance to union development. The materials they produce are easily transported and are guaranteed to draw large interested crowds. The use of audio-visual equipment for general education, health, sanitation, and agricultural improvement will bring to potential union members and others the important message that unions are devoted to the general welfare rather than being merely devices for perpetuating the labor leaders' power and control.

Probably the greatest failing of labor training at the present time is that there is no satisfactory method for determining whether the training has a truly deep effect—in terms of the participants spreading the information they have learned among their fellow workers and union members or of their applying it to day-to-day union tasks. Yet it is almost certain that, when faced with a unique problem back in the field, they have said to themselves, "How would my teacher have handled this?" or, "I wish we had studied this during our course."

In an effort to bridge the gap between the classroom and the shop, it has been suggested that a system of education interspersed with work be developed. A system similar to the Antioch College one—in which the student works for ten weeks and studies for ten weeks, completing college in five years—could be adapted to short-term labor training, permitting the participants to put into practice the lessons learned in the classroom. It would also enable the labor leaders to bring back to the classes the particularly troublesome questions they encountered in their work. In this way, their training would be more closely related to the specific and immediate problems they faced in their daily routine. After all it was to find solutions to these problems that they enrolled in the training courses.

A program of this sort would undoubtedly be prohibitively expensive, if carried on an international level, but it would be quite feasible in national and—even more—in regional or local courses. It could be carried on by international centers providing field work with local unions. Similar to this work-study approach is the use of refresher courses in which the centers bring back certain key students as tutors in subsequent classes. The special course at Kampala for labor educators, organizers, and researchers is a similar effort, open to graduates of the college.

Further activities of this type would be a valuable stimulus to more effective labor education and would ensure, more than any other techniques could, that what was learned at the centers was put to good use and that the centers were solving very real problems. If adopting the entire program is imprac-tical, it is still feasible to provide a closer liaison between the centers' staffs and alumni. Constant exchange of speeches, classroom materials, copies of local laws, new ideas, and notes on the progress of classmates will be of great practical as-sistance to the labor training alumnus and will assure him that he is not alone in his activities. Periodic follow-ups—bringing alumni back to the center or holding refresher courses in the field—would also create the desired continuity.

This consideration of teaching methods is not intended to be a catalog of how to educate labor leaders. Such information is readily available from classic writings on education and, specifically, on adult or worker education. What the discus-sion was intended to do was to point out the danger of rely-ing on the lecture system as the only technique of teaching and to consider the feasibility of other techniques that are calculated to have a greater impact on the students. Which technique is most desirable depends on the problems of the labor training centers, the abilities of the students, and the ingenuity of their instructors.

On the whole, the outlook is encouraging. As more and more of the centers "mature" in handling the increased num-bers of students, they will seek out new techniques for putting their message across. The proof of their adaptability and their desire to meet the needs of their students is there. All of the centers, even the newest, have changed or varied their methods in the course of operations. The rapidity of these changes reflects not only the dynamism of the field of labor leadership training but also the likelihood of effective future expansion.

10. EVALUATION PROCEDURES

A final basis for comparing the activities of labor training centers is the manner in which they undertake programs of evaluation. By such programs, the centers ascertain the reaction of the students to the courses or particular aspects of them, while they are still at the center and/or after they have left. Only in this way can the centers get accurate appraisals of their manner of operation and of their effectiveness in meeting their students' needs. The students are the ones for whose benefit the centers have been created, and they should be given ample opportunity to express their satisfaction or suggestions for improvement.

Certainly they are free to make comments at any time during or after the training, but frequently they are reluctant "to bite the hand that feeds them," or do not want to be considered as the only dissatisfied person in the group. Accordingly, they may remain silent even though the opportunity for comment is available. On the other hand, there may be an occasional malcontent who continually objects to various aspects of the program. His comments are no more indicative of the general student reaction than the silence of the rare person who says little or nothing. What is needed and should be sought are the comments of all the students.

Comment or evaluation may on occasion come from sources other than the students, but probably with less validity because of remoteness from the courses and their participants. Sponsors of the centers, or independent evaluators, may examine the courses and make valuable comparisons with the activities of other training centers. In the absence of means for learning how other centers function, this may be all to the good. But in the last analysis, the students of the courses themselves provide the best gauge for determining whether the centers are providing what the participants need and what will stimulate union development.

Techniques of Evaluation

Evaluations can be carried out by interview or written questionnaire. Although the first permits far greater exploration of a given criticism, it raises problems concerning the participant's willingness to be considered dissatisfied. When the interviewer is a staff member, the student is likely to be less willing to criticize if he is still at the center, and more willing if the staff member talks to him in his own home. Conversely, an independent interviewer has greater likelihood of success if he talks to the students at the center, for he appears as someone to whom the students can confide in anonymity. But unless he first meets the students while they are at the center, it is unlikely that he will have as much success as staff members should he interview in the field. He does have the advantage of being able to ask questions about the students' attitudes toward the faculty, questions that could not be asked by the staff members themselves.

The personality problems inherent in interviews can be avoided in written evaluations, where a series of questions calling for *yes* or *no* answers or short-comment answers are asked. This technique should preserve anonymity (by not requiring signatures) because the student who willingly confides his criticisms to an interviewer may be reluctant to make the same remarks over a signature on a document for all to see. As a result, of course, the staff will not be able to assess the relative worth of the answers in light of their sources. Written evaluations also suffer from the fact that the students can discuss the questions together before filling out the form, so that it is difficult to obtain truly personal views. In the case of evaluations written by alumni already returned home, the main problem is one of getting the forms returned, as anyone familiar with the postal problems in Asia and Africa will testify. And even if they do not sign the questionnaires, the alumni will no doubt restrain their comments because of the comparative ease with which they can be identified through the postmarks or their comments on current status.

Subjects for Evaluation

There is no limit to the number of items that can be asked in an evaluation questionnaire. In general, the questions should elicit the participant's reaction to specific details of the courses or administration—one's favorite course, suggestions for new courses or courses to drop, time allotments for each course, selection procedures, teaching methods, housing facilities, kitchen or laundry service, social facilities, and so on. Questions about the faculty could be worked into either a written evaluation or an interview conducted by an "outsider," assessing the faculty as a whole or each teacher individually.

Some space should be devoted to discussion of the center in general, particularly in written evaluations. While this is unlikely to bring extensive responses, it is valuable as an escape valve for those who wish to unburden themselves in one way or another.

For alumni who take part in an evaluation program, the questions should emphasize the contribution the center has made to their effectiveness as practicing trade unionists. There should be opportunity for comment on field work, alumni publications, refresher courses, and selection of new participants. Other questions should provide information on the alumni's activities and progress—whether they have begun labor education programs, negotiated new agreements, been elected to higher trade union or political offices, and so on.

When to Evaluate

The time for evaluation depends on what type of information is sought. Questions on selection, teaching techniques, subject matter in courses, accommodations, and the like, may be asked while participants are still at the center. Although the answers may be geared to what the participants feel the staff wants to hear, it is possible to gain some true idea of their reactions nevertheless. One or two centers conduct such evaluations as a matter of course periodically during the terms. Other centers provide "exit interviews." This evaluation is much more valuable than those conducted during training because it can cover the entire curriculum and elicit general comments on the course when seen in perspective after it has been completed. There is some difficulty if the evaluation is done just as the participants are ready to walk out the door, as it were: The feeling that they are expected to make the center happy makes it likely that affirmative endorsements of the program will be forthcoming. Comments from participants who have returned home and tried to put their lessons into practice are far more valuable. They are more secure and should be willing to give honest impressions of their courses. While they may have forgotten detailed criticism in the time since leaving the center, that same time-lag will mellow their attitudes.

Extent of the Evaluation

Probably the most comprehensive evaluation program is that of the Asian Labor Education Center, which conducts periodic interviews of its students during their courses and also at the time of their departure. Most of the other centers have not had the resources or manpower to conduct proper evaluation programs, although they would welcome the opportunity to do so. One might expect that evaluation programs by mail could be attempted or at least a series of "exit interviews," but such programs have not been undertaken. As a result, the staffs at the centers must rely on the individual students who wish to talk about the center. This can hardly be called an evaluation program because it lacks the required control and is not necessarily representative of all the participants' views.

Efforts should be made by those centers that have not systematically canvassed their alumni to do so. They could learn of the attitudes of the participants toward the administration, the staff, the curriculum, and the center itself; what the participants have done since their return; and what the students want from the center. With such information, the programs of the centers could be adapted to meet changing needs in labor training.

11. THE IMPACT OF LABOR TRAINING PROGRAMS

Are labor training programs successes or failures? Has one type been more successful than others?

Clearly, not all the programs have been failures. To the extent that they have brought trade-union leaders together from diverse backgrounds, given them a feeling of camaraderie, and taught them some lessons in economics and labor relations, they have made a valuable contribution. But these few benefits do not necessarily indicate that the programs have been "successful." There has undoubtedly been more success—judged in terms of effective graduates—in some courses than others. All the centers have attributes that should be emulated by the others. If there were a clearing-house to permit an exchange of information and techniques, the whole field of labor training would surely profit from it. This volume has endeavored in a small measure to help to meet that need.

Probably the perfect test for determining the success of the training programs would be a detailed sociological-statistical survey of the participants, starting before their attendance and continuing for a certain number of years after. Unfortunately, such a study is not practical; the studies that have been made are limited to the participants' experience during and just after their studies and do not consider their preconditioning or the likelihood of their achieving success even if they were not selected for a program.

Most evaluations of the centers' impact on the labor scene have been prepared by the staffs of the centers themselves and are admittedly biased. The only detailed one made by an external evaluator is the one done by Miles Galvin currently at the Puerto Rican school, which was done before he joined its staff. Although, as Galvin acknowledges, it was difficult to draw general conclusions from the fairly limited exposure to the students he had, his study provides some very helpful guides. I attempted another such study of the Kampala Labor College, through visits to its alumni in their home communities. My impressions were necessarily colored by my interest in the center, previous acquaintance with many students, and the varying durations and place of interviews. My impressions are reflected in the criticisms and suggestions set forth throughout the various chapters of this volume.

From these two independent studies, it is hardly possible to draw conclusions that would be fair to all the training centers. The best way to proceed to judge the impact of them all is through the studies and statements made by the staffs. These views are contained at the end of each of the appendixes in the book.

It is fair to say, however, that by and large, the labor training programs have not produced the results their sponsors would like. This general disappointment reflects the various difficulties discussed earlier—particularly concerning the objectives of labor leadership training—but nevertheless, the dynamism of the centers shows willingness to listen to new ideas and to alter programs to meet new needs. With this dynamism, labor training is continually strengthened and now seems to be on the verge of measurable success.

What has been the reaction of those who have come in contact with the training centers or been students in their programs? The teaching staffs, as distinguished from the sponsors, are uniformly enthusiastic. They acknowledge that improvements could be made but generally are too busy with day-to-day operations to examine the weaknesses, although when the weaknesses are recognized, they are quickly corrected. Despite the staffs' undeniable devotion to their work and to the goals set out by the sponsors of the centers, they are lamentably institutionalized. To permit a broader perspective and to add additional relevant subjects to the courses, staff members must be given an opportunity to travel frequently and visit graduates of the course. The need for this was strongly demonstrated at Histadrut's Afro-Asian Institute, where, for the first two courses, the tutors who worked most closely with the students had never been to the countries from which the students came and could hardly have been expected to provide more than a theoretical education to them, so desperately in need of practical training. At the other extreme is the Kampala College, which routinely sends its entire staff all over Africa between sessions—to encourage familiarity with the students' problems and to assist the students in putting into practice the lessons they have learned.

Perhaps a good opportunity to judge comparatively the effects of the various centers would be in an international meeting of all those engaged in labor training work. There have been some labor training meetings at which the senior administrators of the centers are given an opportunity to meet, but these sessions are generally devoted to formal speeches about the operations of specific centers. There is comparatively little opportunity for down-to-earth discussion, and even less for the associate staff members to exchange ideas or learn of new techniques.

While an international meeting would be of value in improving the operations of the centers, an even greater need exists for regional meetings. They would provide opportunities for the several centers which attract students from the same countries to discuss their common problems in the context of specific personalities and regional or national problems.

Trade union leaders in the countries to which the students return are generally satisfied to have them back. Although some realize that they may have encouraged potential rivals, many others (particularly those who were responsible for selecting the students) assert that the students will make substantial contributions to the development of the unions. The evidence is, however, mixed. In some cases, the alumni of labor training programs are given positions of responsibility, either out of recognition of their new skills or out of fear that they may otherwise seize these or higher positions at the expense of the incumbents. In other cases, they are given positions of only nominal influence or "desk jobs," so as to prevent their challenging the incumbent leaders or developing a mass following.

The greatest impact of the labor training program occurs when the union leader himself is the student. There is little question that he will make significant use of the lessons learned, in order to strengthen his union, his position in it, and his chances for advancement.

On the whole, the alumni of the training centers have made a significant impact on the leadership of their unions. Either they have themselves become leaders, or they have stimulated incumbent leaders to a higher standard of performance. In addition, they have often been responsible for introducing new techniques or facilities they learned about when in training. Alumni have also had an impact on their rank and file and on their home communities by offering courses in worker education at home. One example of this is the Workers' Education Society in Calcutta, established by a Calcutta college graduate with the college's cooperation. The Society, open only to graduates of ICFTU courses (for fear of Communist infiltration), started in 1959 and has since established branches in Gondalpara, Champdani, Rishra, Howrah, Kankinar, Budge, Kidderpore, and Bombay. Two union members have been sent to every national course run by the Calcutta college since 1959. A series of courses in trade union studies are offered on Sundays at the College itself, on: "What is a Trade Union?"; trade unionism and democracy; wages and labor economics; organization and administration; and workers' education. For a total cost of approximately Rs 125 ($26.25), the following number of courses were given by the Society in 1960:

	Courses	Participants
Sunday courses	38	358
Teacher-training courses	2	26
Seminars on current topics	2	145
Forum	1	127

The impact of labor training on the business community is more difficult to judge because such a small number of students have been involved, and it is too early to notice the reaction to them within the business community. Nevertheless, individual examples are there and the centers consider them as adequate testimony to the effectiveness of the training. In one case, a Nyasaland graduate negotiated a checkoff for the employees of all Plantation Association members. In another, an employer was persuaded by his union to install a shelter where employees could wait for buses. In a third, a grievance procedure ending in voluntary arbitration was achieved. While these results are of course creditable and valuable as important steps to recognition of unions as partners in progress, one gets the impression that these instances are significant enough, and perhaps rare enough in their occurrence to justify such reporting back to their tutors. It is difficult to tell if they represent common successes. They certainly suggest that most of the graduates have returned to their unions and have begun the slow hard work of building a democratic union—straightening out mismanaged bookkeeping systems, soliciting workers to join the union, and all the other fundamental chores that must be accomplished before the dramatic *coup* of a wage increase, checkoff, or voluntary arbitration agreement is achieved. There are, of course, those rare instances where management encourages the unions because they are a means to more effective relations with the employees, or because they believe in trade unions as effective tools in a democracy. On the whole, the evidence of progress in this sphere is more positive than negative, and the prospects seem bright.

The impact of labor training programs on government has been discussed earlier. At this juncture, it is evident that the governments of the nations to which participants in union-sponsored programs return are at least wary of the alumni. This wariness is due not to the government's position as an employer of a large part of the organized labor force (for, in fact, the labor officials of most governments are sympathetic to the programs as a means of improving working conditions for the laborers), but, more likely, to political fears. For there is growing evidence that the trade unionists of Africa, Asia, and Latin America are, in contrast to American unionists, likely to develop into outspoken politicians of the European school. Powerful to begin with by virtue of their union following and further strengthened by their labor training (albeit economic rather than political), they are viewed as dangerous threats to the status quo. For this reason, as well as for the economic consequences of higher wages, greater fringe benefits, and, of course, strike activity, there are few governments that welcome the returning labor trainee as a positive constructive force in the building of the country. Hopefully, the labor centers can convince the governments (as the Kampala College appears to have done in Uganda) that cooperation is possible to meet mutual needs, for there should be realization in the government of the constructive values of such centers. In the concluding chapter, I shall consider some of the techniques that might be introduced to attain this objective.

In examining the impact of labor leadership training on various groups, let us turn to the most essential group—the graduates of the courses themselves.

The participants in labor training courses have been universally grateful for the education provided. While this gratitude is expressed most clearly in the evaluation forms they fill out when leaving the centers—and therefore affected by both protocol and politeness—there is other concrete evidence that the students have profited from their courses. Even in one country where the government became antagonistic toward one of the labor training centers, most of the alumni were personally grateful for the training and respectful of their teachers. This gratitude may be primarily for the opportunity given them to attend an institution of education, particularly a foreign one. But there is fairly concrete evidence that the participants have gained substantive knowledge, directly valuable to the practice of labor relations, and are grateful for it. Whether they have made effective or complete use of this knowledge is hard to tell. Certainly, too large a number of alumni have not, particularly among the graduates of the early programs. Yet an increasing and sizable group is making active progress within the unions themselves.

As noted earlier, there has been a paucity of studies determining the career of labor-training participants on their return home. One measure of the impact of labor training on the students in a union-sponsored program may be ascertained from a survey I made of the ninety-nine graduates of the first three courses offered at the Kampala Labor College. It is difficult to relate the students' progress solely to the experience at the college, for undoubtedly many of them would have advanced as far even had they not attended. Others perhaps had the opportunity to advance to higher positions but might have preferred to return to their former union jobs to do a more effective job there. In this brief survey, solely the job progression criterion was used, that is, comparison of the job the union member had at the time of the survey with what he had just prior to his attendance at the college. The subjects had been out of the college a maximum of two years when the survey was taken. Personal interviews were held with forty-seven out of the ninety-nine students, or slightly less than half. Comments on all of them were provided by members of the college faculty, local union and government officials, etc. The results are indicated in the following table:

Post-Program Employment of Graduates of the First Three Courses at the ICFTU African Labor College

	Union, Higher Job	Union, Same Job	Management, Labor Relations	Management, Other	Government	Unemployed or Not Known	Labor Arbitration	Total
First course	21	2	3	3	2	1	1	33
Second course	22	2	4	2	3	2	–	35
Third course	14	5	4	2	3	3	–	31
Total	57	9	11	7	8	6	1	99
Percentage *	58	9	11	7	8	6	1	100

* Rounded off.

As can be seen from these statistics, a total of sixty-six or two-thirds of the graduates remained with the same trade union. Although the number who left the union movement may be a cause of concern to the unions, an over-all view of the situation is not discouraging. One must bear in mind that African unions function in a society with inadequately educated manpower; that the demands for educated manpower are great; and that the opportunities for trade unionists with a high level of formal education are both challenging and lucrative. It is reasonable to expect that employment opportunities outside the trade union movement in private industry and government are appealing. One wonders what a similar study of American unionists who have received specialized training would reveal—in terms of the number going into management. Are the individuals who take such opportunities really wastage, as the unions complain? Perhaps they are, in a narrowly trade-union context. But there is considerable merit to the view that they will make more of a contribution to industrial relations—particularly because they had been trained in, and understand, the value of trade unions and their contribution to the national economic picture. Can these trained unionists be considered to have sold out, when they retain and apply the lessons of democratic trade unionism they were taught at the centers? They were hired by management and government with active knowledge of their backgrounds, and presumably with competent personnel officials, well-versed in union operations and alert to the demand for a constructive labor policy. If, in fact, any of those who do go into government or management use their training to the detriment of labor as a group and against their former union brethren, doesn't the main responsibility rest with the selection process of the center they attended? It is there that the self-seeker should be separated from the devoted trade unionist.

Viewing the Kampala data from this perspective, one can say that 86 individuals, or 87 per cent, have remained in the labor relations field. The remaining 13 per cent is composed of the seven individuals who work in management, but not in labor relations, and the six who fall within the accepted definition of wastage, i.e., making no visible contribution to society whatsoever, either in or out of labor relations.

If such an appreciable number of individuals (in this case, 20 per cent of the total) migrate from the unions to other positions in labor relations, the question must be raised of the reasonableness of the trade unions' training for these positions. Should the ICFTU and its African members be responsible for devoting the funds donated by member unions to training potential antagonists at the bargaining table or government officials who will impose restrictions on organizing the expanding public sectors of the economy? On the other hand, the training centers provide the only available supply of personnel trained in labor relations. Government and management have no other source to tap when staffing their operations in the increasingly important area of labor relations. Even without statistical surveys such as that conducted among the Kampala alumni, more subjective evidence of the value of leadership training is available in all the regions where there are labor training centers. It is manifest by the attitude of incumbent union leaders who fear that the trainee will "bring home the bacon" and perhaps oust them from their presently secure positions. It is manifest by the many local training courses that have been started in the communities to which the alumni have returned—here in the alumni's home, there in a recreation hall. This is perhaps the most hopeful indication of the success of labor training programs, for it shows that not only the procedural lessons have been learned (including educational techniques) but, more important, the substantive lessons. In teaching them, alumni reinforce the material in their own minds and at the same time pass them on to eager union members. During a recent trip through Africa, I noted that courses were taught by the graduates of the most recent Kampala course in eight of the ten countries I visited, and in the other two countries, political factors made such courses highly impractical.

Thus, it can be seen that labor leadership training has influenced the staff of the centers, management and government, the trainees themselves, and the trade unions in the countries from which trainees come. This impact is not measurable in terms of the numbers of students who have completed training, nor the return for the money invested—the measurements currently available are more subjective. They lead to the conclusion that the programs have largely overcome their initial handicaps and that their trainees are now accorded recognition—both favorable and unfavorable, each indicating success, since the sources of these judgments vary. There has been some disappointment that the courses have not had a greater impact, but so far, these have been years for laying a foundation. Now the centers have come to maturity and have adapted their courses more specifically to the needs of their students. There are more trainees now, and they are able to group together for effective action. They have caught the attention of government and management. Above all, their goal of building democratic institutions and traditions has come to be understood by the world at large. The prospects seem favorable for further expansion of the programs and heightened success. Many obstacles remain, as this volume has tried to point out; there are many improvements possible. But once the basic principle is accepted, that these training institutions are a valuable asset in a free society, energy can be devoted to helping them to achieve their goals and to have a more recognizable and affirmative impact.

12. PROSPECTS FOR THE FUTURE

As I have noted throughout this volume, the success or failure of any of the centers must be measured in terms of the goals that were formulated by the sponsors when the centers were inaugurated. Although it is often difficult to reconcile the seemingly disparate and occasionally contradictory objectives of trade-union development and economic development, a basic philosophy underlies the many programs and will provide the foundation for expansion of all such endeavors.

That underlying principle is the desire to educate rank-and-file union members in those fields that are deemed essential to the trade unionists' well-being. Such education is not merely intended to increase adult literacy or as training in community responsibility. It is intended as specific education in areas such as economics, public speaking, union structure, labor laws, etc., which will strengthen the average worker's knowledge of his rights, responsibilities, and security in his work.

At the same time that labor training provides a general labor education, it also helps to overcome the shortage of skilled manpower, particularly in administration. Subjects such as how to conduct meetings, keep union financial records, and administer collective-bargaining agreements are essential to union leaders, regardless of the orientation of the programs' sponsors to trade-union or economic development. If the sponsors of the centers can be impressed with the fact that these common objectives underlie all their efforts, it will become possible to initiate more and similar programs by stimulating new sponsors to enter this field.

The great problem here appears to be the basic division between governments and trade unions as sponsors of labor training programs. Both could be convinced of the similarity of their basic goals and the right of the other to continue teaching in its own way. The divergence in their approach may be controversial, but even the centers most oriented to government do contribute to some extent to the development, independence, and stature of the workers. Yet, it is also quite evident that the unions are probably best suited to provide training for the benefit of the workers and are more likely to be accepted as teachers by the workers. However, the unions do not have the financial resources to train the number of union leaders that are needed and asked for. Although the ICFTU has established training centers on three continents and has financed short-term seminars and programs of international visits, it lacks the funds required to establish comprehensive national programs in every developing country or even to expand regional programs to the extent needed. A graduating group of 80 or 120 trade unionists a year at Kampala (a number that will be doubled when a French-speaking college opens), for example, will not meet the needs of the burgeoning trade-union movement of Africa—particularly when a sizable fraction of that group is absorbed in government and management. Increased financial and material support is required from the trade unions in industrialized countries, if trade unions in developing countries are to meet their goals of responsible leadership. In addition, as noted by the survey of the Kampala graduates referred to previously, there is a tendency for management and government to absorb a sizable number of the union graduates for their own purposes, even though they were trained at union expense and effort.

While labor training, then, is valuable for labor, management, and government, the trade unions continue to bear the burden—occasionally with help from sympathetic governments, but seldom from management. There must be some method by which:

1. Management and government can acquire the trained manpower they need without robbing the unions of their sorely needed leadership.

2. Trade unions can continue to develop skilled technicians for their union building.
3. The centers can be freed of the financial burden of training personnel for management and government.
4. A shared understanding of mutuality of interest, with respect for autonomy, can be developed among labor, management, government, and the public.

The descriptions of curriculums of nine centers studied in this volume * show that there is a certain amount of subject matter taught in both union-supported and government-sponsored programs. Undoubtedly, there are differences in the way the material is approached, but, nevertheless, there are certain elements, acknowledged by all sponsors to be universally important, that could form the basis for a whole new effort in labor education, that is, national schools sponsored by labor, management, *and* government, fashioned after the ILO's International Institute for Labor Studies. Such localized efforts could provide practical training in economics, government, labor codes and legislation, statistical research, bookkeeping, parliamentary procedure, etc. The student body could be drawn from labor leaders, management, and government officials within a given geographical area. The participants would be located together, forced to discuss mutual challenges. In this way, greater respect and understanding could be fostered, which would contribute to harmony in the real world of labor relations confronted after the course was over. The variety in the student body would not only assure vigorous, open, and impartial consideration of the subject matter, but would also make possible the mutual understanding and cooperation that is so essential to satisfactory labor relations. As experience in the industrialized nations has shown, labor and management cannot be fully sympathetic to each other if their meetings and contacts are limited to tense contract negotiations for three weeks each year. Joint leadership training in problem areas could help to overcome the handicap of "coming from different worlds."

* See Appendixes.

Such a program would also meet the need for competent government and management officials in labor relations, a need that is demonstrated by the frequency with which management and government attempt to hire union officials who have had labor-relations training. From the government's point of view, the program would provide it with an uninterrupted source of responsible officials in labor relations, and assist it in its effort to encourage interdependence and mutual cooperation. From the point of view of management, the program would provide trained personnel and the opportunity to develop a stronger voice in determining training programs.

For the trade unions, too, such a program would be desirable. It would provide advanced training in local laws and problems for union officials who might otherwise only have access to regional discussion in the international centers. It would raise the level of the international training centers. It would lighten the financial and administrative burden of training persons who might later become "adversaries." It would encourage an understanding of government and management viewpoints within the labor movement. In a larger sense, it would augment the ranks of government and management officials trained in labor relations. With associates across the bargaining table who are familiar with labor's problems, it would be easier and more harmonious for all concerned.

As the experience of the ILO Institute has demonstrated, such tripartite programs are feasible. The financing could be handled by the government of the nation concerned, but could also come from ILO or UNESCO or perhaps even from the Agency for International Development.

Above all, a tripartite program would give recognition to the fact that labor training is labor's responsibility, that what government programs teach in the field is not necessarily the whole picture. It would avoid the partisan approach offered in existing programs and would stress common concerns. At the same time, the program would teach local and national government procedures, especially in the area of labor relations.

Industry studies of the nature of industrial operations as well as union presentations on the structure and operation of their institutions would also be profitable. Studies of the conduct of meetings, structure negotiations, and analysis of the meaning and impact of agreement provisions are also of value when taught in the classroom rather than in the stress of actual negotiations. Other procedural subjects such as keeping labor statistics, and methods of wage payment would also be of value, for these subjects are intricate and difficult and are often misunderstood or overlooked.

If such tripartite programs could be developed, they would help to fill the great need that now exists to prepare the citizens of new nations for their responsibilities in that essential and dynamic aspect of their national life—labor relations. Present facilities are taxed to their greatest limit and are still only beginning to meet the need. Furthermore, the existing programs fail to emphasize the most crucial lesson of labor relations—that is, the absolute necessity of labor-management-government cooperation. If that lesson can be taught in the classroom calm rather than on the picketline, then the programs will have helped to perpetuate that calm in periods of real stress.

This study has endeavored to point out the overwhelming need for labor training. In some cases, the training is needed to bring labor to a power position of parity, so that there can be a reasonable measure of collective bargaining. In other cases, it is needed to teach union members what their constructive role really is, rather than merely to arm for it. In all cases, as the study has sought to point out, without a strong trade union organization under competent responsible leadership there can be no hope for labor relations harmony or understanding.

It is hoped that consideration will be given to the suggestions made here for means to improve the existing programs. It is also hoped that those programs will be expanded, particularly through the stimulation of alumni activities, the multiplication of local training courses, and introduction of programs for manual skill training. In this way, it might be possible to extend the limited impact of the few training centers that are valiantly trying to meet the world-wide needs.

It is also hoped that government and management officials will look more kindly on labor training programs, and that they will endeavor to cooperate in stimulating existing programs and launching new ones. It is hoped that the expansion of workers' education and union participation in labor-relations training will result in greater understanding of the affirmative role of trade unions. With this understanding, governments, management, and labor will be able to move rapidly and effectively together to the goal of industrial democracy, with the assurance of economic security for all.

APPENDIXES

Appendix A

LABOR RELATIONS INSTITUTE
OF THE UNIVERSITY OF PUERTO RICO

Three main programs are operated by the Labor Relations Institute of the University of Puerto Rico: a Latin American Labor Leadership Training Course; a Puerto Rican Labor Leadership Training Course; and a Program for Labor Educators.

LATIN AMERICAN LABOR LEADERSHIP TRAINING COURSE

Structure

The Latin American program began in 1951 in cooperation with ORIT, the American regional affiliate of the ICFTU. In the original agreement with ORIT, it was stated that:

The general objective shall be to teach the technique of administration of trade unions and of collective bargaining, to give an understanding of the role of the union in society and to allow [sic] the ways in which democracy governs administration of labor relations and labor standards legislation.

Transportation of trainees was financed by ORIT, subsistence was provided by the University, and a two-month observation tour of the United States was offered by the U.S. Government. ORIT continued to work with the Institute until 1953, when the relationship was terminated because of the heavy costs and ORIT's preference for holding similar courses in the Latin American countries themselves. Since that time, the Institute has continued to offer courses for Latin American labor leaders with financial assistance from Point Four and subsequent U.S. Government technical assistance programs. The Institute conducts from three to seven courses a year for periods of six and ten weeks each. Enrollment is kept to a maximum of twenty-five students per course, if

possible. To date, more than 650 Spanish-speaking trade unionists
from twenty-two countries have participated in these programs.

Selection

The statute creating the Labor Relations Institute provides that
no admission requirements be established that would deprive any
worker of the right to avail himself of the instruction offered. But
students must be able to read and write, have proven their leadership, and be active union members. The power to select participants in the international program shifted from ORIT to the U.S.
Government technical assistance programs. At present, the U.S.
Operations Mission in the country concerned is informed of a
course being offered; it in turn informs the national unions, who
tell their affiliates. A list of candidates, two or three times greater
than the number of vacancies, is sent by the unions to the USOM,
which has the right to veto any names on the list. The University
makes the final selection.

Curriculum

The curriculum of the Latin American program aims at ac-
quainting young trade unionists from Latin America with the
principles and techniques of modern labor union administration
and collective bargaining, with the role that democratic unions
play in a free society, and with the bases and consequences of union
policies in the total structure of the economy. It examines the way
in which governments are involved in labor-management relations, and their efforts to settle industrial disputes. The curriculum is designed, furthermore, to stimulate thought and discussion
on the appropriate role that organized labor can play in assisting
the economies of developing nations.

The classroom work is supplemented with field observation.
Classes are given in the following subjects: history of the labor
movement; collective bargaining and labor relations; union organization and administration; labor union journalism and public relations; labor legislation; labor economics; educational methods
and techniques; occupational medicine and safety; cooperativism,
and conversational English.

Teaching Techniques

Emphasis is increasingly placed upon classroom discussions
rather than lectures, although larger classes have necessitated a

partial reversion to lecturing. There are classes for about four hours a day, six days a week, supplemented with field trips. This arrangement enables the trainee to acquaint himself with the Puerto Rican labor union movement, the American and local agencies administering labor-management statutes and protective labor legislation in Puerto Rico, and industrial and labor relations practices in trade and industry. Field trips are held in the afternoons, evenings, and weekends. Students meet with union leaders and workers; visit federation headquarters; attend conventions, meetings, and other union functions; visit labor and government agencies; observe representation proceedings and elections; and familiarize themselves with dispute-settlement procedures.

Evaluation

AID officials have conducted terminal interviews with participants when they leave the United States. Follow-up of the Latin American labor leaders is sporadic, inasmuch as the entire program is financed by the U.S. Government. But, the Institute on its own initiative corresponds with the graduates, and Institute staff members visit them in Latin America.

Puerto Rican Labor Leadership Training Course

Structure

Since 1951, the Institute has also carried on a training program for Puerto Rican union officials throughout the island, and since 1956, in a resident course at the University itself. Initially, the course was three months long, given twice a year, with an enrollment of ten to twelve students. This was later changed to several two-month courses per year. Scholarships of $150 per month are offered to participants. As of February, 1963, 199 labor leaders had taken advantage of this resident program.

The University has conducted night classes, workshops, and seminars at the University and throughout the island at union offices. It also carries on one-week full-time training programs in several parts of the Island in a program that began in 1963.

Selection

Familiarity of the Institute staff with the union leaders in Puerto Rico, and frequent contact at the local union level, has enabled the Institute to handle all aspects of selection on its own. Many of the extension activities are open to all union members and there are no selection problems.

Curriculum

In its domestic program, the Institute employs university professors, union leaders, and government labor officials to teach the following subjects: labor-management relations laws (local and federal); collective bargaining and grievance handling; union organization and administration; protective labor legislation; trade-union journalism and public relations; labor economics; union finance and accounting; cooperativism; social security; industrial health and safety; social and political history of Puerto Rico; and Puerto Rican economics.

Teaching Techniques

The teaching procedures in the Puerto Rican programs are quite similar to those considered above in the case of the Latin American program. Classes are taught by means of lectures, conferences, group discussions, seminars, forums, and by laboratories and workshops. Motion pictures are used extensively, as are other audio-visual aids and techniques. Visits of observation are made to factories and labor agencies and organizations.

Evaluation

The Institute keeps in close contact with its ex-trainees from Puerto Rico, both through its training program for labor unions and through continuous visits of these ex-trainees in Institute offices. There has been no formal evaluation undertaken of those who have completed the training programs.

PROGRAM FOR LABOR EDUCATORS

Structure

In 1962, the Institute inaugurated its third program in collaboration with the New York State School of Industrial and Labor Relations at Cornell University, for training labor educators. The students come from Puerto Rico and several Latin American countries for a ten-week course and are organized in classes according to industry, with two or three Puerto Ricans and seven or eight labor educators from other countries in each. As of May 1, 1963, four courses had been held with the cooperation of the Post, Telegraph and Telecommunications International, the Public Service International, the International Federation of Petroleum Workers, the International Union of Food and Allied Workers, and the International Metalworkers Federation. The University pays for the air transportation of participants to and from Puerto Rico through a grant from the Marshall Foundation. Ten dollars per diem living expenses and education facilities are provided by the University. Participating labor organizations must agree to provide salaries for the trainees on their return and opportunities for them to use their newly acquired training skills.

Selection

Selection in this program is made by the University in cooperation with the sponsoring international secretariat. Every effort is made to assemble homogeneous groups, in terms of age, education, union experience, and employment experience. The following are the basic selection standards:

1. Whenever possible, the chosen candidates are those who have taken part in previous training programs of a more generalized nature or who have experience in labor unions. The object is to permit the Institute to concentrate on methods and techniques of organizing and carrying out programs of workers' education.

2. The candidates for training must have demonstrated leadership qualities, preferably by holding elected office in their union. The Institute wishes to be reasonably sure that the students will be able to return to their unions. It is especially desirable if the students can demonstrate that they enjoy the confidence of their fellow union members to the extent of the latter being willing to contribute financially (even if only in a token amount) to their candidate's scholarship.

3. The sponsoring labor organization must be prepared to certify that it has investigated and is satisfied with the character and reputation of its candidates.

4. The candidates must be intellectually and emotionally mature, yet young enough so that they can continue to serve the labor movement for a number of years.

5. Concerning formal education, while there is no strict re-

quirement other than literacy, it is preferred that the candidates have previously demonstrated their ability to learn in a local training program.

One qualification takes precedence over all others: a spirit of service and dedication. Unionists are sought who will respond enthusiastically to training designed to help them learn how better to help others. Candidates are warned that tours are limited, the training intensive, and per diem allowances minimal, but that the students will be members of a small but uniquely qualified group.

Curriculum

The course of study for each of the four groups which have undergone training to date has varied according to the particular requirements of the students and the industry concerned. For this reason, the Institute insists that the directors of the participating labor unions and International Secretariats personally participate in planning and executing each training cycle. The objective is to train each student as an effective organizer of labor education programs and as an imaginative teacher of the principles of union organization and administration. The curriculum is finally decided on only after interviewing each student and after consulting with his union so that each student's program is tailor-made for his unique environmental, organizational, and occupational problems.

The curriculum for the fourth course, which was completed on April 6, 1963, for the International Metalworkers Federation, included the following subjects: effective communication within the union; problems of union organization and administration; labor legislation; trade unions and development in Latin America; planning union educational programs; union-management relations; introduction to, and supervised practice in, group discussion teaching method; techniques of role-playing and case analysis teaching methods; and, introduction to political science and labor economics. The final week of the course was devoted to practice teaching, with each trainee presenting a 45-minute class on a topic in which he has specialized.

Four afternoons per week are devoted to reading and to preparing written assignments on the week's topic. Special workshops of six hours per week are devoted to skills of speaking and writing clearly, of using audio-visual devices, and of conducting union research.

Teaching Techniques

The trainees learn principally by teaching one another under the guidance of their instructors. Each trainee is required to bring with him his labor agreement, the bylaws of his union, the history of his labor movement, and his nation's labor laws. An attempt is made not only to teach the substantive material involved, but also to prepare the trainee to teach the same material when he returns home. For this reason, detailed teaching outlines are prepared by the students. Each group is familiarized with the methods of planning, promoting and organizing education programs and is drilled in basic teaching methods of adult education.

A typical weekly schedule is as follows:

Monday	Group discussion of week's topic
	Study period
	Special supplementary program (on Puerto Rico, on cooperativism, on the sponsoring Secretariat, etc.)
Tuesday	Group discussion of week's topic
	Study period
	Audio-visual Workshop
Wednesday	Field Trip
Thursday	Group Discussion of week's topic
	Study Period
	Research Workshop
Friday	Group discussion of week's topic
	Study Period
Saturday	Writing workshop
	Speaking workshop

Evaluation

There have not been any complete evaluations of the programs for labor educators. To the extent that the participants have come from the various Latin American countries represented in the Leadership Training Course, they have continued to have contact with staff members and profit from on-the-spot

Latin American Attendance at the Labor Relations Institute of the University of Puerto Rico

Country	Regular Program	Special Six-Week Seminar	Program for Labor Educators	Program for Cooperative Leaders	Program for Women Trade Unionists	Special Program for Dominican Republic	Total
Argentina	—	—	1	—	—	—	1
Bolivia	35	8	2	—	—	—	45
Brazil	8	—	1	—	—	—	9
British Honduras	2	—	—	—	—	—	2
Chile	40	—	—	4	—	—	44
Colombia	126	—	6	—	—	—	132
Costa Rica	20	—	2	—	—	—	22
Cuba	9	—	1	—	—	—	10
Dominican Republic	—	—	—	—	—	10	10
Ecuador	22	92	—	4	—	—	118
El Salvador	48	—	1	—	5	—	54
Guatemala	8	—	1	—	—	—	9
Haiti	1	—	—	—	—	—	1
Honduras	70	—	2	1	—	—	73
Mexico	15	—	—	—	2	—	17
Nicaragua	11	—	—	—	—	—	11
Panama	10	—	2	—	—	—	12
Paraguay	3	—	—	—	—	—	3
Peru	63	—	2	3	—	—	68
Trinidad	1	—	—	—	—	—	1
Uruguay	8	11	—	—	—	—	19
Venezuela	22	—	5	—	—	—	27
Total	522	111	26	12	7	10	688

assistance, and offer suggestions for improvement in the Institute's operations.

Impact

As may be noted on the accompanying chart, there have been approximately 700 participants in the various Latin American programs of the Institute. In addition there have been 800 participants in the programs for Puerto Rican union leaders. In the absence of studies of the activities of the alumni of these various courses, it is difficult to ascertain whether they have had an appreciable impact upon the trade-union movements in their countries. This is particularly hard to determine because of the several other international centers which are operating in Latin America, whose alumni might also be responsible for any recognizable improvement in the posture of Latin American trade unions. Undoubtedly the greatest impact may be expected from those who have taken part in the labor educators' program, for their work will significantly augment the rank-and-file awareness of the importance of trade unions in the political, economic, and social life of the Latin American nations.

Appendix B
ICFTU ASIAN TRADE-UNION COLLEGE, CALCUTTA

Structure

The Asian Trade-Union College, sponsored by the ICFTU and financed by its Regional Activities Fund, was opened in Calcutta on November 5, 1952. The facilities included three rented buildings that housed college offices, a lecture room, a library, a dormitory, and dining facilities. The college subsequently moved to a different location nearby with similar facilities.

The objectives of the college were proclaimed as twofold: to bring together active trade union workers from all over the Asian continent, to help them study and absorb the basic principles and methods of modern trade unionism, and to equip them to do organizational work in their own countries with greater conscientiousness and efficiency; and to train cadres of workers to organize local educational programs in their respective countries. To achieve these objectives, a program was developed at the college for trade-union leaders from ICFTU affiliates in India and throughout Asia. Participants come from Burma, Ceylon, Republic of China, Hong Kong, Japan, Malaya, Okinawa, Pakistan, the Philippines, Singapore, and Thailand. Indian unionists take an active part in the international courses, as well as in local courses that have been developed.

College work is divided among the following programs:

1. International Courses. These are held twice each year for twelve weeks each. An average of twenty students attend, coming from an average of five countries; usually one-half to one-third are Indians. Since the courses are taught in English, a period of instruction before the official course opens is offered in English-

124

language training for those who need it. Recently, it has become the practice to teach the first course of the year as a basic, general course, and to use the second for more advanced consideration of industrial relations, law, labor economics, and collective bargaining. Students are requested to pay the first $70 of their transportation costs and to arrange for the support of their families during their absence. As of March 1, 1963, there had been twenty-one international courses attended by 562 trade unionists from fifteen Asian countries.

2. Indian Courses. These courses, each four weeks long, are taught in Hindi, Urdu, Bengali, and English, and are specifically oriented to Indian union problems. Enrollment is approximately twenty students per course. Students from Pakistan and Nepal also often attend. At least two of these courses are taught per year bilingually in Hindi and Urdu. These courses are given for trade unionists who are unable to devote more than a month to such formal education. The students are requested to pay their own transportation costs and to arrange for family subsistence while away from their homes. Some of the unions offer subsidies to cover these costs. To date, sixteen courses have been held, attended by 341 participants.

3. Short Trade-union Courses. At the request of the national union centers or their affiliates, the college arranges one or two-week courses on local union problems. These are held all over Southeast Asia. They arc usually taught in local languages and are organized with the full cooperation of the local labor unions. Nine such courses have been held in East Pakistan, attended by 387 students. As of March, 1963, sixty-five had been held in eleven countries with 2,017 participants. There were twenty-six short courses held in Calcutta, Bombay, and Nasik in December, 1962, and January, 1963, on the "Role of Trade Unions in the National Emergency Caused by the Chinese Aggression."

4. International Seminars. The college also arranges international seminars on specific problems of concern to Asian trade-union movements. These are held either at the college or elsewhere in Asia, with participants coming from affiliated national centers. The recent emphasis has been on training in worker education techniques, and in gathering labor statistics and other research information. An Asian Seminar on Workers' Participation in Management held in April, 1963, in New Delhi, was attended by

thirty-two students from eleven countries. There have been eight International Seminars with 223 participants.

5. National Seminars. The college also arranges seminars on specific subjects of current importance and on advanced or specialized courses for unionists in a particular industry, at the request of national centers affiliated with the ICFTU. They are often held in conjunction with alumni meetings in a particular country, thus serving also as a refresher course for graduates.

6. Weekend and Evening Courses. These are often given at the college itself but not as part of the official program. They are given for the Calcutta Workers' Education Society, utilizing the college's faculty and facilities. The courses concentrate on training union rank and file rather than union leadership. The subjects taught include organizing a union, the history of Indian and international labor union movements, trade unionism and democracy, and workers' education.

The college maintains a specialized library on subjects covered in its curriculum. As of March 1, 1963, it had a total collection of 4,054 books and 246 current periodicals.

The college is responsible for the establishment of the Workers' Education Center and, since the Center is used as a model, is indirectly responsible for similar centers established elsewhere in Asia. The Calcutta Workers' Education Center was inaugurated early in 1953 as an extension service of the college, to demonstrate the methods and techniques of workers' education to its students. It is a laboratory where new methods and techniques of workers' education may be evolved and tested. The Center is located in the dock workers' section of Calcutta, in a series of small ground-floor rooms behind some local shops. It was initially attacked by competing union groups, particularly by Communists, but in due time developed a large and loyal following. A monthly enrollment fee is collected, and the money is used to provide refreshments. Enrollment is restricted by the physical limitations of the quarters, but a year and a half after its opening, more than 150 workers were enrolled and paying the necessary fees. Attendance, now, runs to 70–80 students each evening of the week.

The headquarters are open all day but there are organized activities only during the evening. The program starts at 7 P.M., with singing of union songs in the local vernacular, followed by a discussion of current events, when the day's news is analyzed. After this are classes in English, Hindi, Urdu, or Bengali, until 9 P.M. From then on, the program varies from evening to evening, with forums, news discussions, skits based on workers' experiences, sports events, and lectures. The members of the Center also divide into special clubs for a particular field or special interest, such as poetry, drama, or music.

In addition to these group activities, the Center has two other innovations. One is the "wall newspaper," consisting of newspaper illustrations with multilingual comments. This is posted daily outside the entrance, and is explained to passers-by during the day by staff members. The other innovation is the wall poster, prepared by students at the college or members of the Center on a particular union story, history of a labor movement, a contract negotiation, etc.

The Center also has a library of several thousand books in English, Hindi, Urdu, and Bengali, for students at different levels of language proficiency.

The Asian Trade Union College also publishes and distributes materials of interest to trade union members. Study guides, for instance, are available in several languages. *The Asian Trade Unionist,* issued in 1958 and again in December, 1960, included articles by the students on the trade unions of their countries, as well as articles on events in international and Asian labor. Another publication, the *Monthly Bulletin,* which began in April, 1961, identifies itself as "a digest of news and events relating to the Asian Trade Union College. Its endeavor will be to serve as a link between the college and its Associates [alumni] and as a medium of communication among the Associates themselves."

Selection and Curriculum

This being the only institution of its kind in Asia for this type of trade union training, the college had to see that as many countries in this region as possible got the benefit of its services. National trade union organizations in the different Asian countries affiliated for each course, and every effort was made to secure representation of the entire free trade union movement in this region. The College also invited nominations from the International Trade Secretariats and nonaffiliated organizations in the region maintaining friendly relations with the ICFTU, the Asian Regional Secretary, and the Director of Education for Asia.*

* *Asian Trade Union College,* ICFTU, Calcutta, 1955, p. 6.

The college seeks a wide range of industrial as well as geographic representation in the student body. Each candidate, whether for a short course or for the full resident course, must meet the following requirements: He must be a bona fide worker and member of a trade union, or a full-time union official; he must pledge himself to serve the trade union movement after completing his training; and, he must have had some general education, including a working knowledge of the English language. In addition, "In the final selection from among the candidates, the College gives full weight to the qualities of leadership of each applicant as shown in his or her past record." *

The syllabus for the first course included the following areas: "What is a trade union?"; union organization and administration; collective bargaining and shop activities; history of the trade-union movement in Asia, Europe, and America; labor legislation; general and applied economics; economics and social problems of Asian countries; political topics; and educational, welfare, and community activities. Later, the following subjects were added: techniques of intellectual work, how to use libraries, conduct social investigations, prepare material for reports, conduct debates, discussions, etc.; statistics; industrial psychology and its bearing on problems of trade-union organization and activities; current affairs; and the meaning of democracy and its relation to trade unions.

Some of the courses were modified during the actual teaching. For instance, the course in general economics changed from a study of the evolution of economic systems to a study of existing systems and aspects of them bearing on the trade-union movement, with particular emphasis on Asian economics and the Soviet and Chinese economic systems. Similarly, the course devoted to political topics enlarged its scope to include detailed examination of problems of democracy, the nature of the welfare state, the U.N. Declaration of Human Rights, and Communism.

At present, there are nine areas covered in the curriculum, each considered in a series of working papers. Here it will suffice to list the areas covered in each seminar, and under them the titles of relevant working papers:

1. What is a trade union?
    a) Union aims and functions

* *Ibid.,* p. 5.

b) Unions and politics
c) Union membership
d) Internal organization of unions
2. Organization and administration of trade unions
    a) Enrollment of members
    b) Union meetings
    c) Union elections
    d) Union publicity
    e) Strikes
    f) Union dues
    g) Collection of dues through union representatives
    h) Union finance
    i) Maintenance of union offices and records
3. Trade unionism and democracy
    a) Definition of democracy
    b) Constitution of a democratic organization
    c) Trade unions' concern with democracy
4. Collective bargaining
    a) Definition of collective bargaining
    b) Procedures and techniques of bargaining
    c) Fringe benefits
    d) Seniority
    e) Union security
    f) Grievance procedure
    g) Wages
5. Industrial-relations law
    a) Legislative practices in different countries
    b) Protection of the right to organize
    c) The right to collective bargaining
    d) Settlement of industrial disputes
6. Labor economics
    a) Wages
    b) Standard of living
    c) Wage determination with relevance to
        (1) Capacity to pay
        (2) Cost of living
        (3) Productivity
        (4) General economic conditions
        (5) Demands of economic development
7. Workers' education

    a) Aims, scope, and content
    b) Forms of programs
    c) Methods and techniques
    d) Evaluation of the suitability of various agencies
8. History of trade-union movements
    a) International movements
    b) National movements
    c) Union constitutions and structures
9. Social, economic, and political developments in Asian countries
    a) Country-by-country analysis
    b) Trade-union positions in these countries.

A few additional lectures are usually arranged on time and motion study; job evaluation; wage incentive systems; industrial psychology; problems of economic development; and workers' participation in management.

The curriculums of the shorter Indian courses and various other special courses are, of course, adapted to the particular needs of the students.

Teaching Techniques

When the college began, lectures and question periods were used extensively, together with lengthy reading assignments. The original system did not prove effective, however, because the students lacked preparation for such formal education and failed to absorb the material. The procedure was changed to a series of discussion groups arranged around formal lectures. Recently, the school changed its technique again, and it now uses a system that is quite unique. The main subjects are divided into subtopics. Each subtopic is treated in a working paper, containing a concise statement of the topic and a list of relevant questions to ask about it. The student is given one of several working papers, which are short statements of a particular subject with a list of questions. He is also given a booklet containing more detailed resource material on the same subject, collected from texts and periodicals. The students read the working papers and notes, and then meet in small groups (from four to six in each group) to study their notes and reading and discuss their findings. In a larger group of ten or so, they consider the questions raised in the working paper which had been assigned to them. These discussions are led by college teachers. The whole working paper is considered in these discussions, and the students are then redistributed into a few small working parties for more detailed consideration of the working paper. Each question in the working paper is considered separately and a separate reporter is appointed for each point. He is responsible for taking notes on the subject during the discussion, listing his subject on the blackboard, preparing a report and presenting it to the general session.

The general session includes all of the students in the course, divided into groups that have all been studying the identical working paper. Each group presents its report, and each is considered point by point. After each group has reported on its particular point, the Director of the college, who presides over the general session, brings out the differences among them, invites comments from the students, sums up the discussion, and adds any information or comment he may think is necessary—in effect, a short lecture on the subject. This procedure is followed for the whole curriculum. On some occasions, there are outside lecturers, usually experts in the field, but only after the preceding procedure has been completed. Graduates of earlier courses also return to the school to give lectures or to serve as assistant tutors for an entire course.

Certain subjects are quite effectively taught in demonstration classes—techniques of collective bargaining and grievance proceedings, for instance.

Forums and panel discussions are also held when trade union leaders or experts on a certain subject are available. Debates and discussions of this type are held for and by the students throughout the course.

Field trips are also used to great advantage to show the students —particularly those from other countries—some of the industrial activity around Calcutta and (on week-long tours) nearby industrial areas. Visits are made to company and union officials, and the students have specific assignments for research or observation. These assignments are all discussed when each student gives a report.

When the college first opened, the course ended with a final examination. Because of language difficulties and the general dislike of formal tests, however, the examination was replaced by a weekly discussion with the student about his work and the introduction of a course-long research project for each student. The students are shifted into groups either of equal ability (as it is judged in the weekly appraisal of his work), or, deliberately, of mixed ability—to assure equal progress in each working group. This encourages fraternization among all the students, permits closer cooperation among the working groups, and makes possible constant examination of the progress of each student. The final week of the course is now devoted to evaluating sessions, where the students present their individual chosen written project on the best way to build their union on their return home. They are also asked for their impressions of the curriculum and teaching, as well as for suggestions for improvement of the course.

The ICFTU Workers' Education Center is another important part of the Asian Trade Union College. Extensively used by union rank and file, it serves as a valuable site for studying and experimenting in various educational techniques that might be adapted to a participant's trade-union needs in his own country. The preparation and use of posters, wall newspapers, charts and the like are readily observable and easily copied. Sets are loaned to graduates of the College for use in exhibitions. Wall newspapers, exhibitions of posters, the library and reading room are all effective devices for teaching labor education. An entire worker education program, is, in effect, available at the center for transfer to other trade-union centers.

An effort is made to continue in contact with the students after they have completed their course. At the end of the program, each student prepares a personally selected project on what he intends to do to build his union when he returns. The staff of the college endeavors to keep in contact with the student to check on his progress in his particular undertaking and to offer advice on his work when needed. The college maintains files on all the students which, though not complete, are a valuable source of information on the impact of the college. *The Asian Trade Unionist* and the *Monthly Bulletin* have also stimulated continued interest in the college and its programs.

Evaluation

The college has not conducted any formal evaluation program among either currently enrolled students or its alumni. It does encourage comments and correspondence from its students, however. Participation of alumni in national courses permits an added opportunity for oral evaluation, although there is no indication that evaluation is an important factor in alumni contact.

Impact

The curriculum and teaching techniques used in Calcutta are among the best offered in any international labor training program. After a decade of experiment, this oldest of international worker education centers has developed an approach that should be a valuable model for all other worker education programs, not only in its teaching techniques, but also in its effective alumni relations, post-graduate work, and grass-roots contact in local education centers. This last tool is a very effective device for accomplishing an essential objective—that is, raising the adult literacy level.

In 1954, in a college pamphlet, ICFTU General Secretary Oldenbrook listed the results achieved in two years as "impressive, although a drop in the ocean" in terms of the need. The Director, V. S. Mathur, listed several of the problems facing the college:

1. The lack of time to secure proper documents from the governments of the participants before the courses begin.

2. Deficiency in language ability of some of the students, despite the requirement to be fluent in English. Special English classes were established to overcome this, and it was urged that greater attention be paid to the English requirement; that students who did not know English well come one month early; and that more extension work be undertaken in non-English speaking countries.

3. Selection process impaired by ineffectiveness of leaders in the participating countries and by delays in the processing of applications. It was hoped that this problem would be solved after there were graduates of the college exercising leadership in local unions. It was pointed out that an increase in the number of short regional courses would meet the demand for more local courses and help in the discovery of suitable students for future international courses.

4. The extensive absence required to attend resulting in unemployment on the student's return. This is considered unavoidable until the unions are strong enough to require management to grant fully paid study leaves. But now it limits the students' ability to work actively in their unions on returning home.

5. Difficulty in maintaining contact with graduates. This failure was due either to the great amount of time-consuming work and responsibility facing the students at home or to depression and

feelings of futility and helplessness in the face of overwhelming problems. Refresher courses and short courses were looked on as methods for stimulating action and improving relations.

6. Lack of sufficient written material in languages other than English for dissemination of trade-union information throughout Asia.

In November, 1962, Director Mathur noted that through the activities of the college:

A sizable group of trained trade unionists have already been created in each country of our affiliates. . . . The international courses . . . and regional seminars have helped . . . in securing better appreciation and understanding of the need and role of trade-union education and have helped in the creation of a better atmosphere for educational work in the different countries. The shorter local courses . . . have also served as demonstrations of methods and techniques of teaching as well as of conducting such courses. . . . They have indeed almost taken the College to those unable to come to it. . . . Though quite a number of trade unionists who came to the College have attempted on their return some educational work, for various reasons not many have been able to initiate or develop any sizable programs in this field. . . . The general apathy and indifference for educational work not only affected proper selection of participants for its courses but also their utilization after their return by the organizations sponsoring them, and thus obviously limited the effectiveness as well as extent and scope of the activities of the participants.*

* Speech delivered on the tenth anniversary of the college.

Appendix C

LABOR EDUCATION CENTER
OF THE UNIVERSITY
OF THE PHILIPPINES

Two programs are operated by the Labor Education Center, a domestic program and an Asian program.

DOMESTIC PHILIPPINE PROGRAM

Structure and Curriculum

The Center began formal operations in 1954 as a joint U.S.–Philippine Government program administered by the University of the Philippines. Its avowed objectives were three: to meet the need for educating workers, officers, and members of trade unions in the principles and methods of free, democratic, and responsible trade unionism; to help promote a more rational and intelligent consideration of problems affecting labor and management in the Philippines; and to help develop an atmosphere of healthier labor-management relations. By 1958, U.S. Government participation had ended, and the program now continues as an exclusively Philippine operation.

Among the projects undertaken by the Philippine program are the following:

1. Weekend Institutes. These are conducted in the field for the rank and file who desire a rudimentary education in trade unionism but who lack the opportunity or the leadership qualities necessary for participation in longer and more advanced programs. As of February, 1963, twelve such institutes had been held with 513 participants.

2. Union Leadership Training Institutes. These more compre-

hensive courses are oriented to practical problems faced by union officials. Each includes instruction on subjects such as trade unionism and democracy, union administration, rights and responsibility of workers under the law, how to run a union meeting, and collective bargaining. By February, 1963, there had been 200 such Institutes conducted for 8,736 union officials.

3. Advanced Institutes. These are offered to union officials who have completed the basic courses. They are conducted as evening courses in various locations throughout the country and last as long as five weeks. Subjects such as collective bargaining, social security, union administration, shop steward and grievance processing, work simplification, and accounting of union funds are considered at an advanced level. By February, 1963, 37 advanced institutes were held for 1,396 participants.

4. Union Education Directors Training Institutes. This program is designed to teach education directors of participating unions to undertake programs adapted to the specific needs of their union and its members. The courses last one or two weeks. Seven such courses have been held with 234 attendants.

5. Trade Union Research Institutes. This specialized course is offered to research directors or unionists responsible for research projects. In the one or two-week program, they are taught specific skills in research techniques and their most effective application. Five research courses have been held to date, the most recent having 16 participants.

6. Resident Labor Training Schools. This school, with the most comprehensive course in the Philippine program, which lasts for two months, is "graduate" training for those who have successfully completed at least two of the short-term institutes. It is the nucleus of the Philippine program and most nearly comparable to the other resident programs considered in this volume. At the conclusion of the thirteenth resident course, 345 labor leaders had participated. The sponsoring unions pay for the travel expenses of participants and subsistence for their families. The University of the Philippines offers scholarships to cover expenses while at the course, which is held in Diliman. In some cases, trade unions have negotiated specific provisions with their employers that provide for compensation to participants while at the school.

Under the program, courses on the following subjects are offered: trade unionism and democracy; international labor movements; collective bargaining; union structure; organization and administration; labor legislation; the Philippine labor movement; economic problems, policies, and programs; nonagricultural cooperatives and credit unions; parliamentary procedure; public speaking and debate; and labor education techniques.

7. Non-labor seminars. The Center also conducts weekend seminars for public school teachers to prepare them for teaching fourth-grade students (the highest general level of education) about unions, and seminars for the police in basic trade unionism and the legal rights and protections granted to unions. Also, during the past year, a Labor-Management Relations Course was held for twenty-five members of a Supervisors' Association in Yupango. These non-labor seminars are unique among the several worker education programs studied here.

To date, over 385 institutes and courses have been held with a total attendance exceeding 15,000.

The Center also has an extensive audio-visual program that prepares slides, film strips, and sound motion pictures. These are used with particular success as an integral component of its field activities. It has developed a sizable library and publication program including among other items a *Labor Education Center Bulletin* for alumni, a reprint series of speeches and articles of interest to Philippine trade unionists and scholars, and a labor bibliography for high school teachers.

Selection

Participation in the courses depends on the level and location of the particular course. The introductory weekend courses are open to all rank-and-file union members. The more advanced courses are generally restricted to those actually involved in the activities discussed—shop stewards, education directors, and the like. In the national courses, selection is made by the staff of the Center with regard to regional quotas and major industrial representation. In addition, the effort is made to include rank-and-file members rather than officials, to encourage the development of leaders from within the ranks. The finances are handled by the sponsoring unions. The Director and staff reserve the final right of selection, subject to the final approval of the Board of Scholarship of the University of the Philippines. The students must have the ability to read and write English; a background free of Communism, totalitarianism, and subversion or willing collaboration with such parties or movements; good character and morals; demonstrated potential for democratic leadership in the union and the community; demonstrated awareness of the mutual interests of labor and management, and of the importance of free collective bargaining in developing a healthy and democratic labor-management relationship.

The courses offered at the Center encompass a curriculum adapted to the specific demands of the participants.

For example, the course for union education directors includes instruction on how to conduct role-playing demonstrations, panel discussions, and skits, and how to use most effectively the lecture, discussion, flannel board, blackboard, posters, charts, field trips, small one-room trade-union museums, and picture collections.

Another example is the Collective-Bargaining Training Institute for Unions in the Manila area, which ran evenings for five weeks in May–June, 1961, and listed the following subjects for discussion: the philosophy of collective bargaining; labor legislation; analysis of contract clauses; contract writing; negotiation of the agreement; administration and enforcement of the agreement; economics of collective bargaining; research; labor disputes—settlement through conciliation and mediation; grievance procedure; the shop steward system; the duties and functions of the Department of Labor; duties and functions of the Court of Industrial Relations; and, the goal of industrial peace.

Teaching Techniques

When the Center first began, emphasis was placed on formal lectures, with some time devoted to discussions. This proved ineffective in sustaining the interest of the students. Since that time, panel discussions with outside experts, seminars, and select study groups to discuss specific issues have been relied on extensively. These techniques have not only led to more student involvement in the subject matter but have also broken through to the more aloof students by group exploration of their points of view and resulting "eye-opening" self-examination. Guest lecturers are relied on a great deal, particularly visiting union officials from the Asian countries. During the past year, ICFTU-Asia and International Plantation Workers Secretariat officials and trade unionists from Burma, Malaya, India, Japan, and Pakistan spoke to and with the students. There has been limited use of non-Philippine lecturers.

Limiting the number of students to the capacity of one DC-3 airplane has permitted the participants to undertake extensive field observation trips to visit union and government labor offices, plants, plantations, and the Center's regional headquarters.

The Center also publishes news releases and a news bulletin and distributes display boards, study guides, course outlines, speech reprints, and elementary pamphlets in English and the local vernacular. The Center serves as a consultative agency, arranging for speakers at labor and management functions, assisting unions in developing worker education programs, and planning and developing union publications. Its audio-visual facilities are used not only to provide motion pictures and film strips for educational shows and tape recordings for radio broadcasts, but also to prepare original films and tape recordings. Its 3,500-book library and research facilities have been used in the preparation of seventeen labor federation histories, issued in pamphlet form, and of reports on collective-bargaining trends in several industries. The Center cooperates with the Philippine Department of Labor, the Social Security System, the Cooperative Administration Office, the Industrial Development Center, the ICFTU, UNESCO, and ILO in projects of mutual interest and benefit.

Evaluation

The only extensive evaluation done at the Center was made under the direction of Mrs. Florida Ruth Pineda-Romero, at the time the Resident Labor Training Officer. Her evaluation of and conclusions about the resident labor training program from 1956 to 1960 were divided in three major areas:

1. Administration and Operation of Union Affairs.

a) Several students introduced the shop steward system or made the existing procedure more workable on their return to their unions.

b) Union leaders realize the need for greater member participation in union affairs. Committees have been created to handle different union functions.

c) Parliamentary procedure has been introduced.

d) There is more active union participation in community affairs.

e) Former students have overhauled their unions' structures to effect an either decentralized or more efficient administration.

f) Union leaders now realize the need to keep members informed about union affairs, especially about financial matters, and now make wide use of bulletin boards, newsletters, and other means of communication. Treasurers and union presidents keep a strict eye on finances.

2. Collective Bargaining Agreements.

a) Labor-management relations have become more reasonable. As one worker said, "Management is not as unreasonable as it originally appeared to me; it has its own valid reasons for doing what it does."

b) One union now encourages an increase in productivity by giving prizes to deserving employees from union funds.

c) Another union has initiated monthly meetings with representatives of management to thrash out matters affecting daily relations.

3. Worker Education. Unions have introduced many of the following measures:

a) Small-scale educational programs with union officers acting as discussion leaders.

b) Utilization of union meetings for educational purposes —such as lecturing on worker education or trade union matters.

c) Cooperating with other educational programs.

d) Accepting invitations to speak or teach in classes conducted on a local or federation level.

In his 1960–61 annual report, Dr. Cicero Calderon, Director of the Center, made the following recommendations for improving the Philippine program:

1. Strengthening the labor relations program for management, police agencies, and other institutions.

2. Separating the research and publication operations.

3. Expanding the field staff by employing field personnel who can organize and conduct courses on their own.

4. Considering qualified members of the staff for University faculty tenure.

Impact

In 1960, Dr. Calderon made the following observations:

1. The Center continues to enjoy the solid support of the trade-union organizations of the country.

2. There has been an increase in workers' education programs developed by individual unions.

3. Emphasis on basic leadership training institutes has borne results but should now be shifted to the training of union education directors and teachers.

4. Trade unions in Manila have only recently awakened to the value of the Center's services and are making increased demands for educational programs among unions in the Manila area.

5. The development of a course in Trade Union Research and the publication of the LEC *Economic Bulletin* have encouraged and trained labor leaders in the use of economic data as a tool for effective collective bargaining.

6. The Asian Seminar on Workers' Education in October, 1958, was the most significant contribution of the Center to promoting workers' education.

ASIAN PROGRAM

Structure

In 1960, the Asian Labor Education Center was established as an international program of labor leadership training, using the hitherto untapped resources of the Asian Economic Development Fund, $372,000 from AID, and a land grant of one hectare from the University of the Philippines (later increased to ten hectares). $50,000 was allocated for the annual budget of the Center. ILO, UNESCO, the Asia Foundation, and similar organizations have given scholarships and transportation grants to students from countries lacking resident AID missions. In addition, $10,000 has been allocated for travel within the Philippines. A new building was inaugurated on January 6, 1960, and the first Asian Labor Leadership Institute began the next day—with twenty-seven students from Burma, Ceylon, Indonesia, Korea, Malaya, Pakistan, the Philippines, and Taiwan. Since this first course was held, there have been six others with students coming also from Hong Kong,

India, Japan, and South Vietnam. A total of 163 have been trained
to date.

Attendance at the Asian Labor Education Center

	First Course	Second Course	Third Course	Fourth Course	Fifth Course	Sixth Course	Total
Burma	2	—	2	2	—	—	6
Ceylon	5	4	9	3	4	—	25
Hong Kong	—	—	—	—	2	—	2
India	—	—	—	—	2	3	5
Indonesia	4	3	2	3	—	—	12
Japan	—	—	—	1	3	—	4
Malaya	3	2	2	2	2	5	16
Nationalist China	1	1	2	2	6	2	14
Pakistan	4	5	1	5	—	—	15
Philippines	6	3	6	5	4	4	28
South Korea	2	—	2	—	3	6	13
South Vietnam	—	1	—	—	1	4	6
Total	27	19	26	23	27	24	146

The Asian program brings trade-union officials to the Philippines
for ten-week courses not unlike the Resident Labor Training School
in the Philippine program. Subjects include: the international
labor movement; contemporary labor problems in Asia; public
speaking and debate; parliamentary procedure; labor economics;
trade unionism and democracy; union administration; cooperatives
and credit unions; labor education methods and techniques; labor
and social legislation; labor-management relations; labor productivity; work simplification; and human relations and collective bargaining.

Selection

Selection of participants in the Asian program is done on a
basis similar to that used for the Philippine program, with a quota
assigned to each participating country. According to the prospectus
of the Asian program, each participant must: understand and
speak adequate English; be a member of a bona fide trade union
organization, preferably in a responsible position of leadership;

not be a member of any subversive organization; be a citizen of the country whose national trade union center nominates him for training; be willing and able—physically, mentally, and emotionally—to travel to the Philippines and reside there for the duration of the course; be able to engage in an intensive seminar and training program and to communicate and otherwise disseminate the results of his training upon return; possess sufficient maturity to provide proper representation for his country, showing ability to understand a foreign culture and to benefit from experience abroad; be in good health; and, preferably be between the ages of 25 and 45 at the time of nomination.

Curriculum

The curriculum of the Asian program is more general than that of the domestic program and is oriented to Asian labor problems in a wide perspective. It includes the following subjects:

1. *Trade Unionism and Democracy.* The course covers the right of workers to organize, union philosophy, objectives, and responsibilities in improving the workers' standard of living and human dignity, the criteria of free trade unionism as expressed in selection of members and officers, avoidance of Communist or other subversive control, the relation of the public interest to union activities, and the reconciliation of trade unions with the legitimate objectives of economic development. The study guide includes "Basic Features of a Democratic Union," by Dr. Calderon; "Trade Union and Democracy," by Robert L. Kinney; "The Basic Faith of Democracy," by Samuel E. Stumf; "Trade Unions: Aims and Objectives," by G. Mapara (ICFTU Asian Representative); "Trade Unions—Romance and Reality," by Professor Benjamin Selekman; "The Role of Trade Unions in a Democratic Society," by Cipriano Cid; and "Labor's Role in Society," by Gordon B. Cushing.

2. *International Labor Movement.* The course is designed to provide familiarity with the historical development and contemporary influence of English, American, Asian, and international labor activity, with particular attention devoted to the structure and functions of the ILO, ITS, ICFTU, and WFTU. The study guide contains a "Discussion Outline on the European Trade Union Movement," by Attorney Luis R. Mauricio; "Social As-

pects of International Trade Union Work," by Alfred Braunthal; "Postwar Developments in International Labor," by David J. Saposs; "Some Facts About the ICFTU," and suggested reading lists on the ILO, the WFTU, and the ICFTU.

3. *Labor-Management Relations.* This course embraces a study of labor-management relations—collective bargaining, negotiations, preparation of contracts, agreement issues, and effective enforcement. Management and labor leaders take part in discussions recounting their own experience in the field. Attention is paid to the use of economic data, the grievance procedure, and the role of the government as employer, mediator, conciliator, arbitrator and administrator.

Among the materials used is a booklet with five speeches by Philippine leaders on labor-management relations.

4. *Union Structure, Organization, and Administration.* This course considers the importance of sound international union structure, and ways to operate a union with the most effective allocation of responsibility and division of authority. It discusses building up membership participation and loyalty, development of leadership, conducting of union meetings, financing and accounting, local educational programs, and strengthening inter-union relations.

5. *Labor and Social Legislation.* The role of the government as regulator of conditions and standards of work is considered with regard to labor relations, social security, minimum wages, protection of women and children, industrial safety and inspection, and workmen's compensation. The objectives, content, and application of such legislation are examined in relation to the conditions in various Asian countries.

6. *Labor Economics.* This course, geared to the economic problems of Asia, includes sections on the economic problems of underdeveloped countries, national income accounting and analysis, money and credit, monetary policy, public finance, fiscal policy, international trade, and labor and wage theory. It deals in greater detail with the subject of Asian labor problems—including the institutional setting of modern labor problems; manpower development and utilization; the supply and demand of labor; types of unemployment and underemployment, theories of employment; conditions and policies of full employment; security against un-

employment; labor and the shorter work-week movement; and economic insecurity in old age, in sickness, or because of accidents. Some attention is also devoted to trade-union research and labor statistics. In general, the course stresses the role of the trade union as a contributor to national economic policy—with special emphasis on problems of the labor force; skill distribution; unemployment; and wages. The economic effect of collective bargaining is also considered, as are labor productivity programs and their benefit to management, labor, and the consuming public.

7. *Contemporary Labor Problems.* This covers some of the basic problems confronting Asian trade-union movements. Students divide into small discussion groups, each one of which concentrates on a specific problem. Among the subjects considered are: factors impeding the growth and development of the trade-union movement in Asia; workers' education and leadership training; union finances; protection of the basic rights of workers to organize and bargain collectively; trade-union unity in Asia; and low standard-of-living and unemployment problems.

8. *Cooperatives and Credit Unions.* This course considers the formation of credit unions; producer cooperatives and consumer cooperatives as group devices for attacking high prices and interest rates; encouraging employee thrift, stimulating cottage industries, and encouraging self-help in solving unemployment and underemployment problems.

9. *Parliamentary Procedure.* The techniques of how to run an orderly meeting with full and free discussion are analyzed. Workshops and mock meetings on hypothetical union issues are conducted.

10. *Public Speaking and Debate.* This covers speech composition; arrangement and presentation of ideas for formal and informal occasions; and suggestions for improved clarity, audience response, and effective argumentation.

11. *Labor Education Techniques.* Each student is encouraged to begin, develop, and evaluate education programs in his own union. Organizational, promotional, and financial problems are considered, as well as the basic philosophy and goals of workers' and other adult education. The role of international agencies and assistance organizations is analyzed, and the comparative value of various techniques and teaching devices are considered.

Teaching Techniques

The techniques employed in the Philippine program are also used in the Asian program. The courses were taught in English for the first four courses; then, simultaneous translations were inaugurated—initially for the benefit of the Indonesian participants.

Evaluation

The U.S. Operating Mission in Manila conducts detailed evaluation programs during the courses and at their conclusion. No evaluation is carried out when the participants have already gone home. Although no formal evaluation has been published to date, certain comments made by the students themselves reflect some of the prevalent attitudes:

1. Training should be increased from ten weeks to three months to lessen the studying pressure; greater contact with local unions should be encouraged at the Center; more time should be used for study groups and less for lectures.

2. Economic theory, rural development, and village aid programs should be stressed.

3. The program was helpful in learning how to organize and build trade unions through effective dues collection, improved negotiating techniques, worker education programs, and organization of difficult sectors such as agrarian labor.

4. The graduates indicated their intention of establishing national trade-union education centers.

5. Information on the development of indigenous industries as a means of economic development and the end of unemployment was valuable.

6. Subjects that should be included or augmented in the course are: trade-union organization and administration; trade-union democracy; parliamentary procedure; public speaking and debate; labor economics; collective bargaining; politics (relations between political regimes and the trade-union movement, as well as the role of the unions in economic development); trade-union ethics; industrial hygiene; industrial psychology; grievance procedures; labor laws of Asian countries; more extensive field trips and English-language training.

In his 1960–61 annual report, Dr. Calderon made the following recommendations:

1. That an evaluation survey be made upon completion of the fifth or sixth regional institute.

2. That scholarship funds be augmented to finance additional participants from countries without U.S. Operations Missions or formal labor programs.

3. That the staff be given an opportunity to visit union centers in participating countries to examine conditions and problems of trade unions and labor relations.

4. That a nine-channel console be added to the audio-visual studio, to permit the local production of film strips with sound.

5. That additional transport facilities be acquired.

In addition to these formal evaluations and recommendations, many people connected with the center and, in particular, with the Asian regional program, have added their personal comments and suggestions for its improvement. Some of them have argued that the course is too short; that too much attention is devoted to the labor and legislative history of the Philippines and not enough to that of other Asian countries; that many students from countries with little educational opportunity suffer from their inability to absorb the material, while those with better educational backgrounds are held back; and that contacts with Philippine labor leaders are too few—particularly on field trips, where most of the time is spent with management officials.

Impact

The Asian Labor Education Center has only a comparatively small number of alumni, but they seem to have a substantial effect in the creation of new labor training centers in their countries. Comments from representatives of management, labor, and the Philippine government indicate general satisfaction with the operation of the program.

Appendix D
ICFTU AFRICAN LABOR COLLEGE, KAMPALA

Structure

The African Labor College, sponsored and financed by the International Confederation of Free Trade Unions, was first recommended at a meeting of the African Regional Trade-Union Conference of the ICFTU in Accra, in 1957. It was decided that the college should cater to the needs of English-speaking trade unionists, who represent the largest percentage of ICFTU-affiliated unions in Africa. Kampala, Uganda, was selected as the site for the college because of its desirable centrality for the English-speaking countries of Africa, its suitable climatic condition, its proximity to Makerere University, its agreeable racial and political situation, and its ready accessibility by air, rail, and boat transportation.

The college was designed to provide trade-union education to union members and officials who previously had no facilities for training in the field. The formal prospectus listed the following objectives:

1. The training of active and prospective trade-union organizers and officials, in order to assist in building up and reinforcing the growth of democratic and free trade unions in the various African countries;

2. The training of trade-union instructors to help spread worker education by organizing and conducting trade-union programs in their own unions and areas;

3. Stimulating and organizing educational programs in various African countries and/or regions and, in particular, industries, the latter in cooperation with the ITS concerned. The affiliated

national centers will be encouraged to institute their own training programs as quickly as possible;

4. Subject to the availability of funds and personnel, to give advice and technical assistance to unions and national centers in the field of organization, administration, collective bargaining, and research.

The college began operations in rented quarters in Kampala on November 3, 1958. It was not until 1961 that it was finally able to occupy its own facilities in a newly constructed college compound.

Financing of the Labor College and its programs has been through the International Solidarity Fund of the ICFTU and by direct trade-union and individual donations. Students are provided with room, board, laundry service, and transportation to and from the college. In addition, they are given a nominal amount of pocket money to meet their personal needs while attending. The provision of a family subsistence allowance is available for individuals with dependent families, if they are unable to arrange for such subsistence from either their own funds, their employers, or their unions. An increasing number of students have been able to arrange for leave with pay from their employers, testifying to the growing strength of the national unions and to the increased respect that the college enjoys in management circles.

The core of the African Labor College is its four-month residential course. To date, it has trained over 250 trade-union leaders from sixteen English-speaking African countries, plus Aden and Mauritius. In addition, the college has made its facilities available for Ugandan and Kenyan worker education programs (as well as for seminars in other subjects, such as cooperatives), when the resident courses are not in session.

Its field activities have grown consistently. The college has held short-term courses at many of the national union centers, taught either by visiting staff members from Kampala or, preferably, by local graduates of the college. In December, 1961, the college began publication of its *Labor College News*, which not only discusses ICFTU activities in Africa, but also covers activities of the alumni and gives information on the subjects taught at the college. There is also extensive publication of study guides, which are distributed to graduates.

From February through July, 1963, the College undertook a special course in research, workers' education, and organization, a course open to both new and old students "whose record at the College and/or work in the field show promise."

Finally, the college has begun a statistical research project to help meet the critical need for labor relations data in Africa. This program, carried out with the aid of grants and personnel from Europe, will serve the needs of management and government, as well as labor, in amassing and interpreting needed statistics on labor laws, wage rates, contract terms, migration and the like. It will help to achieve a more scientific and responsible approach to the factual areas of collective bargaining. From the labor viewpoint, such data will strengthen the otherwise weak trade unions with statistical information hitherto available only to the employers.

Selection

At the present time, selection of participants for the resident course is carried out jointly by the officials of the several national centers and the staff of the college.

According to the former Principal of the college, Sven Fockstedt, the college seeks students with a fairly high and even standard of English, which would enable them to benefit fully from the training program and to communicate without difficulty with their fellow students; with fairly similar background, knowledge, and experience in trade-union work, in order to avoid a situation where some find the courses too advanced and others too elementary; who can easily adjust to a new environment and communal living.

To obtain these students, the college contacts affiliated and sympathetic national centers in Africa, Aden, and Mauritius. It also contacts local units of the International Trade Secretariats. Bearing in mind the need for geographical and occupational distribution within each class, the Principal makes the final selection. Too frequently, internal political demands within a union become a very important factor.

In the first seven courses, the students came from eighteen countries, as indicated in the following chart:

Attendance at the African Labor College

Country	First Course	Second Course	Third Course	Fourth Course	Fifth Course	Sixth Course	Seventh Course	Total
Aden	1	2	2	2	2	2	2	13
Cameroon	—	—	—	3	2	2	—	7
Ethiopia	—	—	—	—	1	—	—	1
Gambia	3	2	1	1	2	2	1	12
Ghana	4	4	—	—	—	—	—	8
Kenya	4	4	5	4	4	4	5	30
Liberia	—	—	—	3	2	2	2	9
Libya	—	—	1	—	—	—	—	1
Mauritius	2	1	1	3	2	2	1	12
Nigeria	4	5	4	3	4	4	5	29
Northern Rhodesia	4	4	3	4	3	3	4	25
Nyasaland	2	1	2	1	2	2	2	12
Sierra Leone	2	2	—	1	2	2	—	9
Somalia	1	1	3	2	2	2	2	13
Southern Rhodesia	—	—	—	3	5	6	5	19
Tanganyika	2	6	4	5	2	4	6	29
Uganda	3	2	3	4	4	3	5	24
Zanzibar	—	1	3	—	—	2	—	6
Total	32	35	32	39	39	42	40	259

An examination of the educational backgrounds of the students in the first five courses indicates that the majority had had some secondary education; nearly a third had had at least four years.

Qualifications for entry into the 1963 specialized course were generally the same as those for entry into the regular courses: a good academic background, or at least five years' active service in unions and good command of English, or, as an ex-student of the college, a record there or at work in the field that shows promise. The applications must be endorsed by the president or General Secretary of the applicant's national trade union, or ICFTU or ITS representative in the area (acting in collaboration with a national trade union organization and on behalf of the International concerned), or the Director of the Extramural Department of the College.

There were thirty-eight students in the 1963 specialized course from twelve countries, as follows:

Cameroon	4
Gambia	1
Kenya	5
Liberia	1
Mauritius	1
Nigeria	7
Northern Rhodesia	5
Sierra Leone	2
Somalia	2
Southern Rhodesia	3
Tanganyika	4
Uganda	4
	39

Curriculum

As at the ICFTU College in Calcutta, the curriculum concentrates on practical trade-union building and techniques for achieving strength in trade unionism.

The course is divided into eight main areas, each containing individual subjects for separate treatment in working papers:

1. *Introduction and Background Information.* The nature and objective of trade unions; basic characteristics of the free labor movement; the trade-union movement in some European countries, the U.S., Canada, and Africa; the ICFTU; and the United Nations and its specialized agencies.

2. *Trade-Union Organization and Administration.* Types of trade unions (craft, industrial, general); structures of unions; functions of trade-union bodies on the local, branch, national, and international levels; organizing techniques; trade-union leadership (prerequisites, demands, responsibilities, and duties); the work of officers; the union constitution and its provisions; trade-union meetings—the importance, function, rules, agenda, and minutes, and the control of the meeting; organizing and keeping union members through service, education, and union security; and, trade-union finance—dues collection, the checkoff, and financial administration.

3. *Particular Problems Facing Trade Unions in Africa.* Trade unions, tribalism, and racialism; problems of African advancement in industry and public services; and, trade unions and politics— the means by which trade unions can influence labor legislation and economic development, and coordination of political action between union leaders and political leaders.

4. *Industrial Relations and Collective Bargaining.* Collective bargaining—its machinery; trade-union negotiations—preparation, techniques, drafting, and contents of agreements; conflicts on agreement interpretation; settlement of industrial disputes, and joint consultation in industry.

5. *Labor Statistics and the Economics of Collective Bargaining.* Common economic terms; introduction to labor statistics—ability to pay, past earnings, and general business conditions; balance sheets; factors in wage determination—supply and demand; use of labor productivity and consumer price index; minimum-wage policy; differential wages and methods of wage incentive—piece rates, bonus rates, and shift payments.

6. *Labor Laws and Legislation.* Legal requirements of trade unions in Africa; legal provisions for conditions of employment and industrial relations; the scope and functions of the Labor Department; and, the role of the International Labor Organization.

7. *African Economic and Social Problems.* Changes in African economic and social life, with a survey of selected Africa economies; economic development in certain sectors, including a study of transport and communication; the role of trade unions in economic development, capital formation, skill formation, and the relation of economic development to political development; problems of migratory labor and immigration; and Africa's economic interdependence with the rest of the world.

8. *Techniques of Communication and Workers' Education.* Public speaking, discussions, reports, official letters, press statements, handbills, placards, union bulletins, and the preparation of such materials; workers' education programs—plans, functions, and techniques; and, the uses of various facilities in the development of workers' education—ICFTU pamphlets and study notes, libraries, and audio-visual aids.

Material on all these subjects, and many more detailed ones, are given to the students for reading prior to the lectures, and for their use in worker education programs on their return home. Among the titles of publications prepared by the ICFTU and distributed to the students are the following: What Is a Trade Union?; Trade Unionism and Democracy; How to Operate Strikes; Model Constitution of a Trade Union; the American Labor Movement; Economic Activities in Africa, 1800–1958; Transition to Industrialism in Africa; Africa's Economic and Social Problems;

the Role of the African Labor Leader; Trade Unions, Tribalism, and Racialism; and, Labor Migration in Africa.

The college also arranges for extra coverage of items of current interest and importance to African trade unionists, and there is a weekly class in political events. Special publications are also issued and discussions held on such matters as the treatment of African students in Moscow, the Casablanca powers, the All-African Trade-Union Federation, and techniques for preventing Communist infiltration and subversion within democratic trade unions.

The 1963 special course on research, organization and labor education was organized as follows:

General Course
1. Economics—a brief but advanced survey and analysis of Africa's practical economic problems covering the following:
    a) Analysis of factors in African economic development during colonial era.
    b) An examination of current ideas relating to economic and social development in Africa.
    c) Economic growth in Africa and the role of planning; public finance and fiscal policy; investment policies; regional economic integration; organized labor; and Africa's international trade.
    d) Africa and the European Common Market and other economic groupings.
    e) The role of the U.N. and other international agencies in Africa's economic and social development.
    f) Economic growth and political freedom in Africa—the role of Free Trade Unions.
2. Trade-Union Studies:
    a) Analysis of the African trade-union movement—its strength and weaknesses.
    b) Trade-union structure in the context of the above.
    c) New approaches to organizing and collective bargaining.
    d) Industrial relations in present-day Africa.
    e) The role of the trade-union movement in developing Africa; self-help activities for trade unions—cooperatives and social insurance schemes for African unions.
3. Political Studies:
    a) Analysis of political developments and trends in Africa and explanations for them; Pan-Africanism and the development of the African Personality as motivating forces.
    b) Analysis of the relations between African and non-African states in the world today.

Special Courses

A. *Research Course*

1. Analysis and explanation of trade-union research—its purpose and value to unions and the community.

2. Union research methods and interpretation of results.

3. Areas of trade-union research:

   a) Interpretation of company accounts and use of various procedures to determine ability to pay.

   b) Analysis of developments and trends in a specific industry.

   c) General economic analysis of the national economy.

   d) Analysis of wage structure and levels in relation to a), b), and c), above.

   e) Investigation of price levels and trends in relation to a)—d) above.

   f) Objectives and norms in economic development vis-à-vis capital investment, labor policy, industrial policy, etc.

   g) Sources of research information.

B. *Course for Education Instructors*

1. a) The meaning and purpose of trade-union education in Africa.

   b) Analysis of the problems facing the African trade-union educator.

2. Methods of Teaching:

   a) Determining the experience, background, and interest level of students as a guide to teaching.

   b) Effective instructional demonstration methods for students having low literacy level.

   c) The use of visual aids in classroom teaching and in general educational promotion.

   d) Practical application of above to teaching on "Our Union," "How We Organize Our Union," "Collective Bargaining," "Union Administration," "The Economics of Our Industry," "Labor Laws in Our Country," "Industrial Relations," etc.

3. Techniques of Organizing Trade-Union Education Programs:

   a) Practical methods of organizing and administering trade-union education programs at national and lower levels; factors to be taken into account—lingual, literacy, and other; deciding on educational strategy—when to run courses for top national officials, shop stewards, or women unionists; the choice of themes for various courses; deciding on the duration of courses and on seminars, workshops, institutes, etc.

    b) Preparation of teaching materials—work schemes, time-tables, teaching guides, study notes, etc., and their use at various levels.

    c) Publicity and public relations as means of promoting trade-union education.

    d) The trade-union educator, the press, and the community.

    e) Trade-union education in relation to adult education and other educational programs in various African countries; making use of other educational agencies.

    f) Demonstrations of practical teaching.

C. *Course for Trade-union Organizers*

  1. *a*) The philosophy and economic and political objectives of the ICFTU and the world's free labor movement.

    b) The structure of the ICFTU and the functional relations between the ICFTU, the ITS, and the affiliated national centers.

    c) The record of the ICFTU in Africa.

    d) ICFTU versus WFTU, IFCTU, and AATUF in historical perspective.

  2. Interesting African trade-union and political personalities—who they are, what they stand for, etc.

  3. *a*) Duties of ICFTU/ITS field representatives as counselors, advisers, and promoters of trade-union organization.

    b) Trade-union diplomacy in Africa.

      (1) Approach to various political situations in Africa.

      (2) Cultivating relations with national trade-union centers.

    c) The field representative—importance of personality factor in developing constructive and cooperative relations.

    d) The field representative and the press.

  4. The field representative and union financial procedures and auditing.

  5. Reporting and analysis of trade-union situations and trends.*

Teaching Techniques

At the outset, the college relied on formal lectures as the main teaching technique. Since then, there has been increased emphasis on smaller classes, and in its new facilities, the college has been able to offer many small classes (10–20 in each), in which much student participation takes place.

While most of the topics covered in the college curriculum are

* Taken from the mimeographed prospectus for the special course, ICFTU, December, 1962.

conducive to treatment in either lectures or small seminars, many others are perfect for the technique of role-playing—particularly subjects like strike techniques. Mock negotiations over agreements are held with the staff acting as management. Do-it-yourself materials are used in teaching bookkeeping, studies of balance sheets, checkoff authorizations, etc.

Although films are not frequently shown in the classroom, they are shown every Monday night to the student body as a whole. This is a project in which the students select the films, screen the programs, and operate the equipment. Most of the films deal with trade-union subjects.

A well-stocked library is available on the campus, but at first, it was so closely protected (as are most libraries in Africa) that it was virtually unavailable to those interested in using it. It subsequently acquired a regular librarian and is now well patronized. Materials are donated by the ICFTU Solidarity Fund, as well as by interested national centers, unions, and individuals throughout the free world. The development of the new research center at the college will undoubtedly expand its library facilities.

In 1960, an extensive experimental program in field teaching was undertaken in Tanganyika by George McCray, Senior Lecturer at the college. Five Tanganyikan graduates of the college were given intensive training in the latest labor developments and in teaching techniques. They, in turn, divided into two teams, each equipped with projection equipment and necessary building material, and traveled to fourteen teaching locations. Over 650 branch chairmen, secretaries, and treasurers of unions were taught (in Swahili) the following subjects: moral qualities for leadership; how to organize workers; collective bargaining; union financial management; and, efficient methods of union administration.

The college is currently expanding this successful experiment to a continent-wide program for rank-and-file trade-union training, endeavoring to spread the teachings of Kampala to unionists who lack the opportunity to attend the college. As a first step, it has translated several of its booklets and working papers from English to local languages, using simplified terminology. Utilizing the diverse linguistic skills of its students, the college can quickly prepare simple leaflets, instructional booklets, and teaching aids in several dozen local languages for use in such extension activities. Translations have been made into Swahili and other East African languages at the college itself, and into other Central and West African languages by graduates of the college. These alumni have pioneered in organizing local courses, often at grave disadvantage to their financial position and their relation with local management and government authorities. Throughout Africa, there are now evening courses offered once, twice, or three times a week as appendages to local trade-union business meetings, and there are also intensive weekend seminars and one or two weekday full-time courses. The graduates of the college have played the key role in launching these programs.

With its new extension program, the college is making its first concerted effort to most effectively utilize the graduates of the college in a continent-wide worker education drive. The faculty meets with graduates of the college in a particular country, region, or community for an intensive review of material and techniques of worker education. Then, using the graduates and local union officials, and perhaps foreign trade-union advisors, it sets up teams to carry on a local education program, taught by local personnel in the native tongue. In East Africa, the facilities of the college itself are used. The program also provides further "refresher education" for the college graduates (as in India at the Calcutta College), and a stimulation of greater camaraderie among trade unionists in a given country or region.

Evaluation

Although no formal program of evaluation has yet been made by the College itself, an informal survey of the graduates of the fourth course was made at the end of their attendance that showed general satisfaction with the curriculum. Out of twenty-one students replying, thirteen chose economics as their favorite course, three trade unionism, and the remainder collective bargaining, negotiations, and labor economics. Out of sixteen students, six selected trade unionism as the course they enjoyed least, three economics, two international relations, and the remaining collective bargaining, labor law, handbill preparation, public speaking, and financial management.

Among courses suggested for incorporation in the curriculum were: How to Study, Geography, Sociology, History, Contract Law, Educational Methods, Arithmetic, and English. None of the students suggested dropping any course from the curriculum.

The diversity of subject matter requested for new courses reflects the Africans' overwhelming desire for educational advancement—particularly those in the labor force who are otherwise unlikely to have the opportunity for further formal education.

Out of twenty-two replies, ten indicated that the selection process should be in the hands of the national centers, five that it should be done by the ICFTU and the college, and the remainder that it should be done by the national centers, together with alumni or college staff and full-time union officials.

The majority of 27 students indicated that more time should be devoted to lectures, discussion groups and film shows, and less to role-playing. A change in the length of the four-month course was suggested by thirty students, thirteen of whom wanted it to run a full year, fifteen to run for six months, and two for five and three months, respectively.

Thirty-two students, in unsigned questionnaires, held the majority of the five staff officers then teaching to be very good. Only one faculty member received a vote of poor (from two of thirty-two students).

Impact

In view of the absence of any training facility for trade unionists in Africa before 1958, it is understandable why the college has been as enthusiastically accepted by African trade unionists. It is even fair to conclude that it has had an affirmative impact on the labor-relations scene—judging by the extent to which local trade-union training programs have developed and, perhaps, from the ICFTU strength that was evident in its conflict in 1961 with the All-African Trade Union Federation on the issue of national center disaffiliation from international trade union groups, and from its determination to construct a similar college in West Africa for French-speaking trade unionists.

Finally, there is evidence from the survey of the graduates of the first three courses. As the chart reproduced in Chapter 11 shows (see p. 103), after a maximum of two years away from the center, 58 per cent of the graduates were holding a higher trade union job, 9 per cent were holding the same job they had prior to the course, 11 per cent were working for management in personnel positions, 7 per cent were working for management outside the labor field, 8 per cent were working in government or active politics, 6 per cent were either out of work or unaccounted for, and 1 per cent was in labor arbitration. It can be concluded that 78 per cent were in better positions—a valid indication of the impact of the Kampala College on labor relations in Africa.

Appendix E
INDIAN GOVERNMENT WORKERS' EDUCATION SCHEME

Structure, Selection, and Curriculum

As a result of a study sponsored by the Ford Foundation and an ILO survey of existing worker education programs in India, this program was established in 1958 by the Indian Government, with the support of trade unions, universities, and employer associations. The Central Board for Workers' Education in its prospectus for the Scheme proclaimed the objectives:

In any democracy, the effectiveness of individual participation is ordinarily conditioned by the strength of the organization through which he has of necessity to function. The organization catering for workers in a democracy is their trade union. If industrial workers are to play their role properly in the affairs of the country, they should have strong, well-organized, and well-informed unions run on constructive and responsible lines in the interest of the workers and of the country at large. . . .

Once the need for special schemes of workers' education in India is established, the next question is, what agency should undertake it? It is the practice in advanced countries of the West for the trade unions themselves to undertake this responsibility and that would be the ideal position. But in India, the unions lack the financial resources and organizational facilities required. The government, therefore, decided to give a lead in the matter.

Government assistance to trade unions in conducting worker education programs includes cash grants, for maintenance expenses in operating the facilities, and equipment grants, for purchasing furniture, libraries, audiovisual aids, and other equipment. These supported activities:

Shall as far as possible conform to the standards and curriculum and syllabus laid down by the [Board] for the programs directly administered by it. These shall be subject to the approval of the Society and the education programs undertaken shall be on a purely objective basis. . . . Instructors shall be persons who have successfully completed the Society's training course for Teacher-Administrators.

The program is administered by the Central Board for Workers' Education, an autonomous body constituted by the Government of India in the Ministry of Labor and Employment. Membership on the Board consists of the leading trade-union centers—AITUC (All-Indian Trade Union Congress, once the dominant trade-union group and now Communist-controlled), INTUC (Indian Trade Union Congress, non-Communist and ICFTU-affiliated, the union wing of the dominant Congress Party and the largest trade-union center in India), HMS (Hindi Mazdoor Sabha, Socialist-oriented and ICFTU-affiliated), UTUC (United Trade Union Congress, a small group of left-wing splinter unions, primarily dissident Marxist groups); universities; the Government; and employers' associations.

The program functions on three levels: training of Education Officers, of Worker-Teachers, and of the rank-and-file.

Education Officers are selected to undertake centralized training in a diversified curriculum and are then assigned to act as teachers and administrators of the program at fourteen regional centers, where they teach the Worker-Teachers. The Education Officers are selected by the Central Board.

When the Education Officer course first began, it attracted 600 applications through advertising and 350 through employment exchanges through the Indian Government's Directorate General of Resettlement and Employment. Sixty-seven of the 100 individuals in the first two courses were selected from the ranks of those holding second-class Master's degrees in economics and allied subjects, who also had an intimate knowledge of planned industry operations and obligations under existing labor laws. The remaining thirty-three were selected from the participating trade unions. The group was given a five-month training course during which they spent several weeks at each of the participating national trade union centers. By the time the second course was completed in April, 1961, the sixty-seven students chosen from the universities were assigned as Education Officers to the fourteen regional centers, but none of the trade-union–sponsored candidates was either assigned as an Education Officer or given support in his own union's educational programs.

The syllabus for the Education Officer course includes the following subjects: workers' education—aims, purposes, details, literature; the modern industrial community in India; central labor problems —labor economics, plantation labor, maritime and dock labor, mines, etc.; trade unions—history, purpose, function, constitution, organization, administration, financing, and propaganda; union federations; employer associations; international organizations; labor legislation—principles and problems, history in foreign countries and India, factory acts, Industrial Disputes Act, Minimum Wages Act, Trade Union Act, Employment Act, Workmen's Compensation Act, Maternity Benefits Act, Shop and Establishments Act, Employees' State Insurance Act, Provident Fund Act, Plantation Labor Act, Mines Act, etc.; industrial relations—history, settlement of disputes, collective bargaining, settlement machinery; wages—theory, methods of payment, standardization, incentive systems, cost-of-living allowances, bonuses, nature of current demands; social security; employment and training—employment exchange, recruitment, training within industry, technical education; industrial welfare—health, hygiene, safety, welfare schemes and funds, industrial housing; industrial discipline and workers' participation in management; cooperatives—history, legislation, types; productivity; labor statistics; the second Five-Year Plan; the international labor movement; the Constitution of India; departments of government; and family planning and population problems.

At the Worker-Teacher level, the Education Officers teach individuals selected by the Central Board's Regional Committees. The Regional Committees vary in their composition, but in all cases they include representatives of the four national unions. On the Calcutta Regional Committee, there are university representatives but none from government or management.

The Regional Committee selects individuals with leadership qualities from the local work force (some are nonunion members). The employers pay released-time wages to those selected for the three-month course. The Worker-Teacher trainees are provided with free room and board; if they are away from their home cities, they are also given transportation to and from the center, and weekly tours to various industrial locations. As of March, 1963, 2,598 Worker-Teachers had been trained at the fourteen centers.

It is at this level that the program has its greatest impact, for it is here that it reaches those who will be directly responsible for teaching vast numbers of factory, business, and agricultural workers. There is no doubt that the lessons learned by the Worker-Teachers and then taught by them are valuable to all concerned.

The curriculum for Worker-Teachers gives little, if any, attention to the negotiation, collective bargaining, grievance procedure, or strike techniques, while great emphasis is placed on the Five-Year Plans, discipline in industry, productivity, and cooperation with management.

The curriculum includes the following courses: worker education—origin, history, etc.; Five-Year Plan—concept, role of workers in it; the Second Five-Year Plan; history of development and industrialization in the West and in India; general labor problems; wages; productivity; discipline in industry—importance, grievances, Code of Discipline; worker participation in management—history, joint consultation; Trade Unionism—in India, Asia, England, Soviet Union, and U.S.A., purposes, functions, constitution, administration, finances, publicity, field work, and ILO, WFTU, ICFTU, roles in economic development; industrial relations; social security; cooperatives in India; labor legislation; labor statistics; employment and training—unemployment and underemployment, recruiting techniques, needs of particular states, training within industry; industrial welfare and safety; departments of government; history of India; unity of India; the library movement; population problem; and, sociology.

At the rank-and-file level, the Worker-Teachers conduct classes where they work for an hour or so at the end of the work day. The courses are generally four months long. The Worker-Teachers, paid for their regular job by their employer, receive a bonus from the Government for teaching the course. It has been a practice for Education Officers from the Regional Centers to sit in weekly, and sometimes for management representatives also to take part.

During January, 1963, 710 classes were in operation; 46,146 workers had been trained; and 16,153 workers were still in training. The curriculum at this third level is virtually identical to those used in the higher levels and need not be reproduced here.

Teaching Techniques

Techniques of teaching used include: group discussion, role-playing, debates, seminars and lectures. In the final portion of the courses, additional time is devoted to role-playing, discussion, drama, mock conciliations and adjudications. Trade-union and management officials, productivity experts, and representatives from various embassies give lectures during the second month.

The daily schedule used during the training of Education Officers and Worker-Teachers generally is as follows:

10:30–11:00 A.M.	News Discussion
11:00–12:00 NOON	Educational Administration
12:00 NOON–1:00 P.M.	Group discussion
1:00–2:00 P.M.	Lunch
2:00–3:00 P.M.	Lecture
3:00–4:00 P.M.	Lecture
4:00–5:00 P.M.	Worker-Teachers give their views on the course, trade-union work, etc.

The teaching procedure varies from center to center. At Bombay, for instance, the Education Officers attend two hundred 1¼-hour lectures; eighty lectures by visiting trade unionists, management, or government officials; eleven 2-hour debates; ten 2½-hour seminars; thirty hours of practice in leading a discussion; forty hours in preparing charts, graphs, etc.; 32 hours of role-playing; and 28 hours in skit films. For five weeks, the students were attached to trade unions full time. They also spent ten days with employers and took ten excursions to industrial establishments.

Evaluation

To the best of my knowledge, an official evaluation program has never been undertaken by the sponsors of the scheme.

Impact

By virtue of its government financing and geographical distribution, this course is the largest educational effort in labor training. Some concern has been registered by representatives of the Indian trade unions that participation in this course, with its inducements of financial aid for teaching afterwards, has siphoned off support for and participation in the Asian Trade Union College in Calcutta, which is strictly trade-union oriented. They note the damage that may be done by the Communist unions' involvement in the program, and point out that it does not teach trade-union building—that the students will never know what those lessons should be. They argue that it is merely a mass program to bring the unions into line in support of government and management in economic development.

Defenders of the scheme point out that no trade-union program could possibly reach as many individuals and inform them of their rights; that the unionists are free to join other educational programs instead of this one; and that this program encourages labor-relations harmony, with the full support of all the national unions.

Appendix F

HISTADRUT'S AFRO-ASIAN LABOR INSTITUTE, TEL AVIV

Structure

In 1960, the Afro-Asian Institute was formally launched by Histadrut, the General Federation of Jewish Labor in Israel, with the following expressed objectives: "to provide trade union leaders, cooperators and executives of government offices dealing with related branches, or with economic development, with an opportunity for studies and research." * After the first course, which included both cooperators and trade unionists, it was decided to restrict subsequent programs to single groups, and accordingly the second course was confined to trade unionist participants.

The Institute is financed by Histadrut itself, and was helped at the outset by a scholarship grant from the AFL-CIO. In May, 1963, the British TUC announced a grant of £2,000 to finance additional scholarships for one year.

In the first course, held between October 18, 1960, and March 21, 1961, there were approximately seventy students (half trade unionists and half cooperators) from the following countries: Chad, Congo (Brazzaville), Dahomey, Ethiopia, Gambia, Ghana, Ivory Coast, Kenya, Liberia, Malagasy, Mali, Nigeria, Northern Rhodesia, Sierra Leone, Togo, Uganda, Upper Volta, Burma, India, Japan, Nepal, and the Philippines. They were divided into French-speaking and English-speaking classes. Each had its own tutors and was, in turn, broken up into tutorials for union members or cooperators.

After the first course, cooperators were assigned to rural agricultural schools for specialized training.

The second course was primarily for trade unionists, with

* Prospectus of the Afro-Asian Institute, Tel Aviv, 1960.

167

only a handful of cooperators enrolled. Sixty-three students participated, from May 16 to September 6, 1961, from the following countries: Central African Republic, the two Congos (Brazzaville and Leopoldville), Ghana, Ivory Coast, Kenya, Liberia, Malagasy, Nigeria, the Rhodesias, Senegal, Sierra Leone, South Africa, Chad, Ceylon, India, Nepal, the Philippines, Singapore, and Thailand. The students in this course, too, were divided into English-speaking and French-speaking classes and smaller tutorial groups.

As of April, 1963, three more courses had been held, with participants from the following additional countries: Basutoland; Cyprus; Iran; Malaya; Swaziland; Surinam; and Zanzibar. During the first three years of its existence, the Institute had been host to 353 students from forty countries.

The Institute devotes a considerable portion of the student's time to field trips in Israel—visits to Histadrut settlements and industrial sites. These trips are intended to provide the participant with a thorough view of the comprehensiveness of labor activities within the country.

The faculty of the Institute is selected from the University of Tel Aviv and Hebrew University, and teach their subjects in both French and English. They are assisted by a staff of six resident tutors, also taken from academic life.

In 1962, the Institute undertook to provide special five-week programs for graduates of the ORIT Center in Mexico City.

Selection

The prospectus for the Institute states that:

A secondary school education or its equivalent will be required of all students, that preference will be given to candidates, both men and women, actively engaged in trade union or cooperative movements, or in governmental employ in related fields. In exceptional cases, the educational qualification may be waived at the discretion of the Board of Governors, provided that the candidates have had a wide practical experience in the fields concerned. Participants will be required to have sufficient knowledge of either English or French. Tuition, board, and lodging will be provided without cost to students by the Institute. Students, or their sponsoring organizations, will be responsible for the cost of travel to and from Israel and for pocket money during the course.

This prospectus is sent to national trade-union centers throughout Asia and Africa. There is some direct contact with the Institute by interested applicants, but the bulk of recruiting is handled either directly by Israeli unionists with their counterparts or, more generally, through the good offices of the Israeli Foreign Service in embassies abroad. Through the latter, the Institute has been able to develop a relationship with national union centers whether or not those centers are in contact with Israeli trade unionists. This testifies to the unique role of the Histadrut, which, although it is primarily a trade union, has elements of management and government built into it.

Candidates are interviewed by officials at the local Israeli embassy, and final selection is in the hands of the Board of Directors of the Institute. There have been occasions when the Board has vetoed a recommended student and asked to have a more acceptable person nominated.

Curriculum

The prospectus for the first course listed the following programs of studies: (1) Sociology and Cooperation—theoretical and historical introduction, forms of cooperative enterprise, cooperative law and management, cooperation in developing countries, the cooperative movement in Israel, and three weeks of field work in cooperative settlements; (2) Labor Economics—basic concepts of economics; theories of wages, problems of unemployment, and collective bargaining; (3) Sociology of Trade Unions—history of trade unionism, trade unions in developing countries, trade unions and labor enterprises in Israel, world labor movements, and thirty-day field trips to industrial enterprises; (4) Economic Development—planning and investment policy, problems of agricultural development and industrialization, and training of manpower; and, (5) three weeks of individual training in various enterprises. The classes total 310 hours.

The double orientation of the first course toward both cooperation and trade unionism necessitated a very general and theoretical approach to the problems of both groups. In view of the weak educational background of most participants and their desire for practical suggestions on how to build cooperatives and trade unions in their countries, it proved best to amend the curriculum in the second course to emphasize a more practical approach to trade-union problems and to transfer the responsibility for training cooperators to some of Histadrut's agricultural programs. The second course was reduced in time by one-third of its total class length, all subjects being cut accordingly, particularly those dealing with cooperation. Classroom consideration of the Israeli land, people, and economic and social structures were expanded, while six weeks of field work in cooperative and collective institutions was reduced to a few short visits. Despite the exclusion of cooperators from the second course, the study of cooperatives remains a substantial item in the curriculum, accounting for one-fifth of total lecture time.

The curriculum for the second course was as follows: Israel's land and people; labor economics—trade-union studies and industrial relations, social security, economics: basic concepts, and labor economics; development—economics of development, industrialization, and management of manpower in the development of countries; cooperation—theoretical introduction, cooperative institutions in Israel, and collective settlements in Israel.

In subsequent courses, the emphasis has continued to be upon development problems in new countries, cooperation, the labor movement in developing countries, and trade unionism.

Teaching Techniques

During the first course, there were approximately 300 lectures given during four morning classes. In the afternoon, the two language groups each split into a section for trade unionists and a section for cooperators. Evenings were devoted to varied cultural and entertainment activities, including visits to private homes, theaters, folk dances, concerts, and the like, and to reading assignments in preparation for the next day's lectures. Field trips occupied an average of one day per week. The daily schedule for the first course was as follows:

A.M.	8:15–9:00	Lecture
	9:15–10:00	Lecture
	10:30–11:15	Lecture
	11:30–12:15	Lecture
P.M.	3:00–4:30	Study with Tutors
	5:00–6:30	Study with Tutors

During the second course, the number of lectures was reduced from 300 to 105. This meant one lecture from 8:15 to 9:45 A.M. and a second from 10:15 to 12 noon. Study groups led by the tutors were held for three hours each afternoon. In addition, four days were spent at a Kibbutz; four days at a Moshav Shitufi, six days in observation and field study; and fourteen days on excursions to Galilee, the Negev, Haifa, Jerusalem, Tel Aviv, and Lahish. A few trips were made to study trade unions in the private sector of the economy. Four or five evenings per week, as well as Saturdays, continued to be devoted to general cultural activities, including lectures on general subjects (such as Mrs. Golda Meir on history of Arab relations, and a Hebrew University professor on the Israeli rocket launching). Songs, folklore, dances, films, visits to museums and exhibitions, sports, meetings with local people, and Hebrew lessons occupied the evenings.

Evaluation

To the best of the author's knowledge, there has been no evaluation program undertaken, among either the participants or the alumni.

Impact

Although suffering from the wide geographical distribution of its participants and from the emphasis on cooperation, it is undoubtedly true that the Israeli efforts in labor leadership training are making a substantial contribution to trade-union activities in Africa and Asia. The good reception that the Africans and Asians enjoy in Israel, and the visual evidence of economic development in an emerging country such as Israel, makes the lessons taught even more poignant. Judging from conversations with Africans and Asians who have been to the Israeli courses and with students while they were in attendance, it is evident that the courses are practical, make an impression on the students, and have an impact on their activities when they return to their homelands.

Appendix G
ICFTU INTER-AMERICAN RESIDENTIAL INSTITUTE FOR LABOR STUDIES, MEXICO CITY

Structure

ORIT, the Inter-American Regional Organization of the ICFTU, was founded in January, 1951. The following year, it began a program of labor leadership training at the University of Puerto Rico. The first course, with six Latin American labor leaders, lasted seventeen weeks. From 1951 until 1961, the Labor Institute at the University offered four courses lasting four months each, with a total attendance of fifty students. In addition to these programs, ORIT has conducted many seminars in Latin American countries, often with the participation of the International Trade Secretariats. Such seminars have been held in virtually all countries affiliated with ORIT and have ranged from weekend courses for local officials to month-long seminars for more than forty students from thirteen Latin American countries. Special seminars were offered in 1963 for women trade unionists and young workers. Also, a correspondence course is offered, which has been taken by more than 500 union members.

On April 2, 1962, ORIT launched its Residential Institute for Labor Studies in Mexico, with the initial aim of training teachers and, then, of training organizers, youth leaders, labor journalists, and researchers. The Institute has an experimental laboratory that catalogs material, prepares syllabi for courses given in affiliated national centers, and produces films and other audiovisual aids. The Institute will assume jurisdiction over existing ORIT correspondence courses. As of April 1, 1963, the Institute had completed three courses and graduated 110 participants. There were forty-three students for the second course, coming from Brazil,

Bolivia, Ecuador, Colombia, Chile, El Salvador, Guatemala, Honduras, Mexico, Panama, Peru, Paraguay and Uruguay. There were representatives sent by UNESCO, the Inter-American Miners Federation, and the Public Service International. On completing their studies at the Institute, the entire group went to Israel for five weeks at the invitation of Histadrut. The third course consisted of thirty trade unionists from thirteen Latin American countries. They came from eighteen different industries and trades, among them were: bakers, bank clerks, barbers, cement workers, communications workers, electricians, meat packers, miners, railroadmen, printing tradesmen, taxi drivers, and textile workers.

Selection

Students are nominated by affiliated national union centers, preferably after having completed local seminars offered by ORIT, with the understanding that the national center will promise to use the person trained as a national or regional director of education when he returns.

Curriculum

The resident course runs for two months. When it was first offered, it was divided into two parts: general economic, social, and political problems, and trade-union education, with particular emphasis on educational techniques. In the second course, the approach was altered to integrate the general subjects with the educational techniques. Emphasis was placed on journalism. The curriculum for the second course, held in 162 sessions, was as follows: *Orientation*—international institutions, principles of economics and industrialization, agricultural problems, productivity and automation, social security, cooperatives, democratic institutions, militarism, dictatorship, and popular political movements, Communist tactics, imperialism, and history of the international union movement; *Worker Education*—methods and techniques of teaching, program planning, adult education, union organization, collective bargaining, relation of the unions to the community, administration and trade-union accounting, parliamentary procedure, labor legislation, wages and job evaluation, programs for young workers, programs for women workers, grievance procedures, forming an education committee, techniques of training teachers, organization of peasants' unions, and international union organizations; *General Culture*—labor journalism, public speaking, research and bibliographies, and editorial style.

Teaching Techniques

Approximately three-fourths of the course time at the Institute is devoted to teaching educational techniques. The course stresses learning by doing, and has many discussion groups and practice teaching sessions. Work is done in teams of students headed by a faculty member, and great reliance is placed on audio-visual techniques. When lectures are given, they are forty-five minutes long, followed by thirty-five minutes of questions and answers.

As an example, the course on collective bargaining was conducted in the following manner: The course was divided into four subtopics: (1) preparing the negotiators; (2) preparing the members; (3) legislative aspects, and (4) preparing public opinion. Each of these subtopics was presented in brief introductory lectures (lasting 20–30 minutes), followed by discussion for an equal period of time. The students were then divided into working groups, each of which considered the subject for 2½–3 hours, approaching the subject from their own local or national viewpoints. After five sessions of this kind, a sixth session was held—a panel discussion to review the entire topic.

Evaluation

The Institute has weekly evaluation seminars at which the students and faculty discuss their attitudes toward the proceedings of the preceding week. This permits the faculty to keep abreast of student thought and of student opinion on effectiveness of the course. It also permits the students an outlet—a chance to demonstrate their progress.

At the end of the course, the students fill out a written questionnaire, giving their impressions on various aspects of the Institute and its educational program.

Impact

Although only eighty students have been graduated from the Institute, there are indications of some impact already. Reports from the alumni of the first course indicate that 80 per cent have undertaken active educational programs in their unions. ORIT has assisted them with educational materials and, in some cases, with financial aid.

Appendix H
AMERICAN INSTITUTE FOR FREE LABOR DEVELOPMENT, WASHINGTON

Structure

For several years, the Post, Telegraph, and Telecommunications International Secretariat ran a training program at Front Royal, Virginia, at which Latin American labor leaders were given three months of classroom labor training. These students were then subsidized by the PTTI for the following nine months, during which time they were expected to organize the workers and negotiate checkoffs so that they would become economically self-sufficient and no longer need outside financial assistance.

The successful results achieved by these trade unionists on their return home led the Executive Council of the AFL-CIO to appropriate, in August, 1960, $20,000 for the development of a long-range program for education and training of Latin American union leaders and workers. The American Institute for Free Labor Development was created on May 29, 1962 to administer this program. It is governed by a Board of Trustees composed of Latin American leaders, AFL-CIO officials and North American business and public figures. Trade unionists constitute a majority of membership on the Board. Funds supporting the Institute come from foundations, labor institutions, and public and private sources. The Agency for International Development provided $250,000 to ease the financial strain of the Institute during the first year.

The objectives of the Institute are expressed in its January, 1963, prospectus as follows:

1. To strengthen and develop effective trade union leaders to be not only competent in normal union functions and activities, but also to be able to understand and interpret to their fellow workers the complex economic and political problems facing their countries.

175

2. To create a leadership based not on the concept of the class struggle, but on the constructive role labor can play with other segments of society, including management, to raise their living standards while at the same time strengthening the values and acceptance of the democratic way of life.

3. Training programs that stress quantity consistent with high standards of quality, with emphasis placed on the "multiplier effect," that is, the selection of people for training who have potential for training others. . . .

6. To strengthen the relations and understanding between all free trade unionists of the Western Hemisphere.

In the pursuance of these objectives, the Institute seeks the advice and cooperation not only of local trade-union organizations, but also of regional groups affiliated with international free labor organizations and the various International Trade Secretariats active in the inter-American field.

The main program of the Institute involves training approximately 100 Latin American trade unionists per year in the United States, in a three-month course held in Washington, D.C.

A limited number of internships, for approximately nine months, are provided for those participants who successfully complete the course. Seven-month internships are also provided to receive additional training abroad. These internships enable the students to provide a full-time service to their fellow workers, while still under the guidance of the Institute.

The first course at the Institute, consisting of two classes, started on June 18 and ended on September 14, 1962. One class was composed of twenty-three participants from English-speaking countries of the Caribbean area; the other comprised twenty Spanish-speaking participants from Central America, Venezuela, and the Dominican Republic. The second course, with thirty-seven participants, started on October 1 and ended on December 20, and included students from Costa Rica, Argentina, Chile, Panama, Bolivia, Peru, Ecuador, Colombia, Surinam, Trinidad, and Venezuela. The third course consisting entirely of Brazilians, began on January 28, 1963, with an enrollment of thirty-three students.

The plans of the Institute also envision field educational activity.

Regional and/or national labor training projects are being established in Latin America and the Caribbean area under the direction of the Institute, with the cooperation of national or regional trade-union organizations. The Institute furnishes technical assistance and shares in the cost of running these local projects. Some are run by the Institute on a contract basis with AID, the latter assuming the entire cost. These local projects offer short-term training programs on labor leadership and union administration, serve as a major channel through which graduates from the Institute as well as qualified U.S. and Latin American experts can be utilized in labor education programs, and also serve as a source of candidates for the Institute's future training programs in the United States.

Training projects are already under way or scheduled in Ecuador, Peru, Colombia, Brazil, Argentina, Central America, and Jamaica. It is expected that graduates of the Institute's three-month program in the United States will offer considerable cooperation in the establishment of these projects.

In addition to its teaching programs, a Department of Social Projects was established at the suggestion of the Labor Advisory Committee on the Alliance for Progress. This Department assists free trade unions of Latin America in establishing low-cost housing, credit unions, cooperatives, workers' clinics, vocational and adult education centers, and similar institutions. However, unlike the Institute's other program, which seeks financial support from foundations, labor unions, and other private sources, the Social Projects Department relies entirely on the Agency for International Development for its funds, on a project basis.

The staff of the Institute is currently composed of six trade-union members, four of whom have college training. In addition, there are lecturers and counsellors who work with the students in smaller groups, many of whom come from Latin America.

Selection

Participants are selected by the staff of the Institute in cooperation with local federations or with ORIT and the International Trade Secretariats. Governments take no part in the selection process.

The staff seeks participants who have had experience in trade unions—middle-level administrators, not presidents or the rank and file. There are no educational prerequisites—which seems to cause some difficulty in gearing the level of the course to the abilities of each student.

Curriculum

The curriculum for the Institute is as follows: (1) *Orientation* —cultural orientation, history of the American labor movement, international labor movement, and the International Labor Organization; (2) *Techniques of trade-union administration*—techniques of organizing, types of trade-union structure, collective bargaining (negotiation strategy, types of union security, grievance procedures, labor-saving devices, problems of automation and productivity, case studies of labor-management cooperation), and trade-union finances; (3) *labor education*—techniques of teaching (conferences, lectures, and audio-visual aids, etc.), preparing labor education seminars and planning programs, and trade-union public relations; (4) *field trips*—two, each one week long, including visits to union headquarters, factories, universities, etc., emphasizing points of mutual interest to hemispheric labor movements; (5) *dangers and safeguards for democratic labor*—Communism (theory, global strategy, trade-union strategy, techniques of trade-union penetration, and case studies), fascism and other forms of totalitarianism, political manipulation of labor organizations, and defense tactics; (6) *trade unions and the Alliance for Progress*—concept of the Alliance for Progress, agencies of the Alliance for Progress, and labor's participation in the Alliance for Progress; (7) *democratic labor in a modern society*—trade unions in a developing economy, free enterprise vs. state ownership, and labor as a social force in economic development; (8) *legislation and economics*— labor in the European Common Market, International Trade and Tariff Agreement (GATT), and U.S. labor legislation.

Teaching Techniques

Prime emphasis is placed on lectures, but there is time devoted to smaller counselling or discussion groups and field trips. Postcourse tours of five to ten weeks are provided for 10 students per course, to Germany, Italy, and Israel.

Evaluation

The Institute has not as yet developed any evaluation procedure. Staff members do make frequent trips to the countries from which the participants come and discuss their training and its relevance to their work, but no formal evaluation has been made.

Impact

The Institute is unique in that it not only trains unionists for organizing work, but then subsidizes them while they develop strong union structures. It uses the most direct approach to the basic problem of union building of all the centers. The Institute is still too new for any objective assessment of its impact, but it appears likely that it will lead to a rapid expansion of trade-union membership. When graduates of this Institute work together with those of the Puerto Rican and ORIT programs, there will probably be an appreciable increase in local union training efforts as well.

Appendix I

INTERNATIONAL INSTITUTE FOR LABOR STUDIES, GENEVA

Structure

The International Institute for Labor Studies was established by vote of the Governing Body of the International Labor Office on March 1, 1960. It was intended, in the words of Director General David Morse, to be:

An institution for higher social studies in Geneva which could be a central point of impetus and a source of new ideas for the ILO's worldwide educational work and effort. To this center might come workers, managers, and government servants who have already acquired a certain experience in their work and whose careers may lead them to positions of greater responsibility in the future. They would mingle for a time with students of social affairs, with every opportunity for discussion and exchange of experience in an atmosphere of academic freedom. The aims of the center would be to improve the capacity for understanding and dealing with social questions particularly labor management relations.*

Under the terms of the 1960 Resolution, the Institute:

Shall have as its aim the furtherance of better understanding of labor problems in all countries, and of methods for their solution, notably by: (a) providing educational facilities for the study of labor problems, including the organization of seminars and conferences and of teaching in relevant subjects; (b) arranging for discussion of labor problems between persons having responsibility and practical experience in the field of labor policy as well as others having a special knowledge of such problems; (c) encouraging the study of labor problems at the Institute and in other institutions which can contribute to a better understanding in this field; (d) collecting, digesting, and dis-

* International Institute for Labour Studies; Establishment by the Governing Body, ILO, Geneva, 1960, p. 263.

seminating information concerning new developments in the study of labor problems and encouraging, coordinating, sponsoring, and publishing new research in this field, in support of the educational programs of the Institute.

The Board of the Institute is composed of thirteen members appointed by the ILO Governing Body, including representatives from the Governing Body, "persons of outstanding international experience having a knowledge of educational and labor problems who are not members of the Governing Body," and the Minister of Education of the Republic and Canton of Geneva. They serve for staggered three-year terms, in their individual capacities and not as representatives of their governments or organizations. Their principal task is to prepare a program and budget for the Institute.

The Institute operates as an entity separate from the ILO, although physically located immediately adjacent to the ILO's Geneva headquarters. It is to be financed through revenues to be derived from a special $10 million endowment fund created by contributions from governments, employee and employer associations, and individuals. As of January, 1963, more than $3 million had been donated to the endowment, including contributions from thirty-seven governments. In addition, the Institute receives subsidies from the regular ILO budget, and has also received contributions in the form of scholarships. The income from the endowment provides for operating expenses to meet the estimated budget for 1962 (the first year of operation) of $214,000 and for 1963, of $290,000. Each annual budget is reviewed by the Governing Body. All travel costs and expenses for participants are paid by the Institute, on condition that the students continue to receive their regular salaries.

The Institute also has an Advisory Committee to advise its Director on programming questions. It is made up of persons appointed (one each) by the Director General of the ILO, Secretary General of the U.N., Director General of UNESCO, and the University of Geneva. The Director of the Graduate Institute of International Studies of Geneva is a member. In addition, there are members appointed by the Board "from among educators, recognized specialists in the field of labor studies and others whose experience would qualify them."

The staff of the Institute numbered approximately six for the first course, but it expanded immediately thereafter. In addition, many visiting professors and other qualified persons come on a short-term basis to deliver lectures, lead discussions, and the like.

The first study course, for thirty students, was scheduled for September 17–December 7, 1962, and the second for September 16–December 6, 1963.

The Institute anticipates increasing its courses from one to three or more per year by 1965.

Selection

The prospectus for the Institute contains the following section on Selection of Participants:

The course will be composed of thirty participants selected from the ILO's member States. Candidates must be sponsored by their employing organizations who must undertake to continue the payment of their salaries during their absence. Only in exceptional circumstances will individuals not so sponsored be considered. The essential qualifications are:

    a. good educational background and understanding of economic and social questions;

    b. several years' experience in labor questions;

    c. the holding of responsibilities at a fairly senior level, relating to the formulation or implementation of labor policy;

    d. good working knowledge of English or French.

No quotas are allotted to government, management, or trade unions, and the result for the first course was that about five students were from management, twelve from government, and twelve from workers' organizations. Selection was made by the Director.

A university education is preferred as background but is not a strict requirement. Six or seven of the participants in the first course had no more than a secondary education. Participants in the first course came from twenty-eight countries—nine from Africa, seven from the Middle East, four from Europe, three from South America, and two from North America. Their average age was 35. Seven were lawyers. Seven others were economists, and four were graduates of education courses.

Curriculum

The lecture schedule for the first course included the following subjects, in the order of their consideration:

First Week. Characteristics of economic development; Switzerland and Geneva; state and private enterprise in economic development; the place of the traditional sector in economic development.

Second Week. Health and population and economic development; international economic aid; international technical aid; international trade and its relations to planning and development; social background of economic development; mobilization of public support for a development program; manpower planning in the U.A.R.

Third Week. Employment objectives in economic development; trade unions—structure, organization, and functions; appraisal of investment projects.

Fourth Week. The cost of education and training; manpower problems in Latin America; rural employment; the elements of human resource development planning and the integration of manpower planning with general economic development programming; management problems in labor relations in the developing countries.

Fifth Week. Role of the state in the development of industrial relations; functions of trade unions in developing countries; workers' education; social security—comparative review of national systems and plans and development in underdeveloped countries.

Sixth Week. Methods of collective bargaining; contents of collective agreements; prevention and settlement of labor disputes; representation of workers' interests; labor and economic development; basic principles of the organization of labor in the U.S.S.R.

Seventh Week. Planning in France; wage policy and economic development; incentive wage systems; the economic development of Israel; employers' organizations.

Eighth Week. Labor statistics; the Histadrut; the U.S. industrial-relations system; population pressure and employment opportunities; sociological aspects of educational planning.

Ninth Week. Safety organization in industry; organization of occupational health services in places of employment; prevention of occupational diseases; balance between demand and supply of manpower; workers' participation in management in Yugoslavia; labor and development problems of Burma; wage differentials; management development and economic growth.

Tenth Week. Long-term projections of manpower needs; employment services; attitudes to mechanized work, especially of labor drawn from the subsistence sector of the economy; aspects of change induced by alterations in the rural socio-economic structure and the pull of industry and city.

Eleventh Week. Poland's economic development and certain labor problems in the post-World War II period; vocational guidance; problems of labor administration, including labor inspection, with reference to Africa; forecasting labor supply; mobilization of manpower.

Twelfth Week. Problems of vocational training; some African experiences in planning to promote employment; manpower planning in Eastern Europe.

Of the sixty-one lecturers who participated in the first course, thirty-six were ILO employees and six were on the Advisory Committee, Board, or Governing Body. The remainder were affiliated with other labor-relations organizations.

Teaching Techniques

The schedule provides for one lecture a day, from 9:30 to 10:45 A.M., with simultaneous interpretation. From 11:15 A.M. to 12:30 P.M., seminars are held. From 2 to 5 P.M., the students study in private and work on projects and written assignments.

The working languages of the first course were French and English. (There were seventeen English-speaking and twelve French-speaking participants.) Two seminars were conducted in English, the third in French.

Some time during the course is devoted to visits to local industry, followed by discussion. The final two days are devoted to a recapitulation and a consideration of the students' comments.

In 1963, a research program will be started.

Evaluation

The course is too new to have organized an evaluation study.

Impact

The Institute is the only international center that brings together representatives of labor, management, and the government for free exchange of ideas, and it assures that at least some perspective on other sectors of the economy is gained by all the participants.

This, in turn, undoubtedly affects the participants' attitude when they return to their home countries and normal tasks. It can hardly be expected that there will be any direct stimulation of trade unions resulting from attendance—except perhaps in the case of the trade-union participants—but the atmosphere of the Institute will most assuredly contribute to more peaceful consideration of labor problems, and thus perhaps assist in the improvement of labor relations in participating countries.

INDEX

Adoula, Cyrille, 12

African Labor College, Kampala, 35–36, 55, 64, 66, 67, 81, 98–99, 102, 103–5, 148–60

Afro-Asian Labor Institute, Tel Aviv, 37–38, 57, 67, 71, 83, 99, 167–71

Algeria, 18, 19

All-African Trade-Union Federation, 154, 156, 159

All-Indian Trade-Union Congress, 162

American Institute for Free Labor Development, 39–40, 46, 47, 64, 67, 175–79

Antioch College, 89

Argentina, 122, 176, 177

Asian Trade-Union College, Calcutta, 33–34, 35, 55, 64, 66, 85, 87, 124–34, 152, 158

Audio-visual aids, 34, 88–89

Austria, 18

Basutoland, 38, 168

Bolivia, 122, 172, 176

Brazil, 122, 172, 176, 177

British Honduras, 122

Burma, 33, 35, 38, 124, 138, 141, 142, 167

Cameroon, 7, 36, 151, 152

Central African Republic, 38, 168

Ceylon, 33, 35, 38, 124, 141, 142, 168

Chad, 38, 167, 168

Chile, 122, 172, 176

China, Republic of, 33, 35, 124, 141, 142

Colombia, 122, 172, 176, 177

Congo (Brazzaville), 38, 167, 168

Congo (Léopoldville), 12, 38, 168

Cooperatives, 11, 23, 24, 168, 169–70

Costa Rica, 122, 176

Cuba, 122

Cyprus, 38, 168

Dahomey, 38, 167

Dominican Republic, 122, 176

Ecuador, 122, 172, 176, 177

El Salvador, 122, 172

Ethiopia, 36, 38, 151, 167

Finances of labor training centers, 59–61, 110

Fockstedt, Sven, 150

Galvin, Miles, 97–98

Gambia, 36, 38, 151, 152, 167

Germany, 18

Ghana, 36, 38, 151, 167, 168

Guatemala, 122, 172

Guinea, 12

Haiti, 122

Hindi Mazdoor Saba (HMS), 162

187